THIS BOOK BELONGS TO:

DECORATING SIMPLIFIED:
The Roth Method

Cakes and Techniques by Lawrence M. Rosenberg
Instructions Edited by David Gamon
Photography by Bart J. DeVito

An Allen D. Bragdon Book

SMITHMARK

This book is dedicated by Larry Rosenberg to his mother and father for all their love and support, and to Bobby and Herman Bosboom for their love and help in making his dream come true.

acknowledgements

David Gamon, who coaxed out what Larry knew about decorating cakes, researched what he did not know, and wrote the text; Carolyn Ringland, who designed and decorated the cookies in the "Creative Cookies" chapter with extraordinary skills and fertile creativity; Allen Bragdon, who conceived the idea for the book, asked Larry to participate in it, assembled the professional staff to execute it and provided its creative innovations; Stephanie Schaffer who laid out the pages with charm and clarity; Paris Fried, for her help in testing the recipes; David Munn, for his Chocolate-Raspberry Cake; Jon. M. Cory for his Tofu Icing recipes; Gabriel's Flower Shop in New York City; Mercedes Cea; John Carley; Rose Beranbaum; Bart DeVito, Chris Leone; John Seebach; and Mr. Laszlo Roth;

design and production

Allen D. Bragdon Publishers, Inc
252 Great Western Road
South Yarmouth, MA 02664

Editor in Chief—Allen D. Bragdon
Writer—David Gamon
Art Director—Stephanie Schaffer
Cake Design—Larry Rosenberg
Cookie Design—Carolyn Ringland
Cake Photography—Bart DeVito
How-To Photography—Chris Leone
Jacket Design—For Art Sake, Inc.

This edition published in 1995 by
SMITHMARK Publishers Inc.,
16 East 32nd Street,
New York, NY 10016.

SMITHMARK books are available for bulk purchase for sales promotion and premium use. For details write or call the manager of special sales, SMITHMARK Publishers Inc., 16 East 32nd Street, New York, NY 10016; (212) 532-6600.

ISBN 0-8317-1187-6

Printed in South Korea
10 9 8 7 6 5 4 3 2 1

AUTHOR'S INTRODUCTION

The Roth Method, as presented in this book, is an illustrated version of the courses we teach at the Roth Institute of Cake Decorating in New York. It simplifies traditional procedures. It shows how to create original effects. It reduces the chances of making common mistakes that could ruin a cake you had worked long and hard on.

It's using the cardboard tube from inside a paper towel roll when it'll do just as well as a store-bought candy dough former. It's baking creative cakes in baking cylinders you make from empty cans, instead of buying factory-made specialty pans.

It is clear, step-by-step instructions for making a rose that you can follow and that get results. It's simple, common-sense techniques like freezing a cake to help get the better of crumbs, and using a water mister to keep icing from sticking to your spatula while frosting a cake.

Funny though it may sound, I never would have learned how easy cake decorating can be if my students hadn't helped me. They questioned why I did things in certain ways, why I used some of the tools I did, and they forced me to slow down and explain techniques I had been using for years. Little by little, their questions forced me to simplify, to eliminate unnecessary steps, to work out ways to get the same results faster and with less chance to make mistakes.

Simplicity and common sense are only part of the Roth Method, though. Another part is some new ways we have worked out to create effects that advanced and commercial cake decorators can use—how to color and form a dozen long-stemmed chocolate roses, for example.

And the part of our method that I am most proud of is the high quality of the results it produces, even for people with a little talent but almost no prior training. The methods I show you are ones I use myself, when I make and decorate cakes for my own friends and clients.

I use a prepared cake mix to save time now and then, just like everyone else—but not always. I love to roll up my sleeves and put together the natural, flavorful ingredients that produce that unmistakable home-made taste and texture. I've included some of my favorite cake recipes for you to try out too.

L. R.

CONTENTS

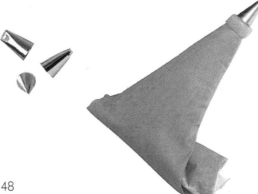

Chapter 1

Happy Birthday, kiddo, from an old flame.

LET'S START WITH BUTTERCREAM

Buttercream is the perfect icing to add a rich, creamy taste and texture to your cake. It's fun and easy to work with, too.

The basic ingredients of buttercream icing are confectioners sugar, water, and butter, margarine, or vegetable shortening. It may strike you as odd that an icing called buttercream may contain no butter at all. All buttercreams have a creamy consistency and a butterlike spreadability, though, so a butterless buttercream is not such a paradox as it may seem.

The bottom border of the "sweet 13" cake on the previous page is made of puffs (tip #2-B) and star flowers (tip #21, and tip #21 for the dot in the middle).

You'll find out how to make puffs and stars in this chapter. The small leaves beside the star flowers are made with a #349 tip. The royal icing chapter shows you how to make them. The top border is made with more puffs and star flowers, all with a #21 tip, and a little delicate stringwork (see the wedding cake chapter to find out how to make stringwork). The rosebuds on top are made with a #104 tip (and a #3 tip for the stem and sepals). The royal icing chapter shows you how to make them. The bow that holds them together is made with a #104 tip.

Buttercream made with shortening, while lacking the flavor of butter, has a very long shelf life, need not be refrigerated, and possesses all the other advantages of dairy product-free food. It's also easier to work with than real butter buttercream, since shortening is less temperamental than butter: it won't get as hard if it's cold, or melt as fast if it's warm. The obvious advantage of real butter buttercream is its taste. If you want, you can substitute margarine for the butter called for in a buttercream recipe, but it won't taste like real butter buttercream, and it'll still be tougher to work with than shortening buttercream.

I usually tell my students to *frost* their cake with All-Butter Buttercream, for flavor, but to do the trickier piped-on decorations with Butter-Shortening Blend or Butterless Buttercream. When just practicing, use Butterless Buttercream. Here are the recipes:

All-Butter Buttercream

6 cups confectioners sugar, sifted
2 cups room temperature sweet butter
¼ cup water
2 tablespoons clear vanilla
Pinch of salt

Measure all ingredients accurately into a large mixing bowl; blend them first at low speed, then mix at high speed 5-8 minutes with an electric mixer, pausing periodically to scrape the icing down from the sides of the bowl.

Refrigerate until ready to use, and restore to room temperature before frosting or piping onto your cake.

Buttercreams containing butter must be refrigerated at all times when not in use. They'll keep up to two weeks if kept in an airtight container in the refrigerator.

Butter-Shortening Blend

6 cups confectioners sugar, sifted
1 cup room temperature sweet butter
¾ cup solid shortening
2 tablespoons water
2 tablespoons clear vanilla
Pinch of salt

Measure all ingredients into a large bowl, and blend them for 3-5 minutes with an electric mixer, pausing to scrape icing from the sides of the bowl with a rubber spatula.

Refrigerate until ready to use, and restore to room temperature before frosting or piping.

Basic Butterless Buttercream

6 cups confectioners sugar, sifted
1 ⅓ cups solid shortening
2 tablespoons water
2 tablespoons clear vanilla
Pinch of salt

In a large bowl, blend all the ingredients with an electric mixer for 3-5 minutes. Pause to scrape the icing from the side of the bowl, then mix for an additional minute. Refrigerate for 10 minutes before using. This Butterless Buttercream will keep for up to six months out of the fridge if stored in an airtight container.

Icing must be the right temperature for it to have the proper consistency for use. Beating the icing raises its temperature, so freshly-made icing should always be refrigerated 15 minutes or so before using. Conversely, always re-beat icing or let it sit out for a half hour or so minutes or so after refrigeration, to restore it to room temperature.

Flavored Variations

You can make flavored variations of any of the basic recipes given above. Here's how:

For a *chocolate buttercream,* add ¼ cup sifted unsweetened Dutch-process cocoa, plus 2 tablespoons water added to the water already called for in the recipe. Mix this with the other ingredients as indicated in the method of the recipe.

For a *double chocolate buttercream,* add ¼ cup melted unsweetened chocolate.

To make other flavors, substitute the desired essence (lemon, almond, etc.) for the vanilla in the basic recipe. If you have a butterless buttercream, you can use artificial butter flavor for a buttery taste and to mask the flavor of the shortening. Keep in mind that a colored flavoring agent will change the color of your icing.

Coloring Your Icing

You can use liquid, paste, or powder colors in buttercream (see the appendix to find out where to buy them). If you use more than just a dash of liquid color, though, subtract from the amount of water called for in the recipe according to the amount of liquid color you add. Paste or powder color will not affect the consistency of your icing, so you can add it after the icing is mixed without adjusting the other ingredients in the recipe. For more information on colors and coloring agents, see the "Colors and Coloring Techniques" section in the appendix.

1. Fold down the end of the bag to form a cuff, and use a spoon or spatula to fill the bag with as much icing as you need.

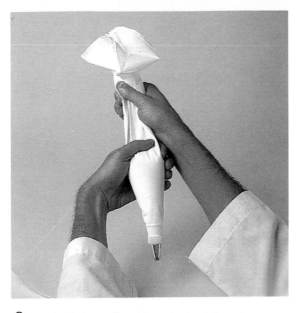

2. Unfold the cuff, and push the icing down towards the tip.

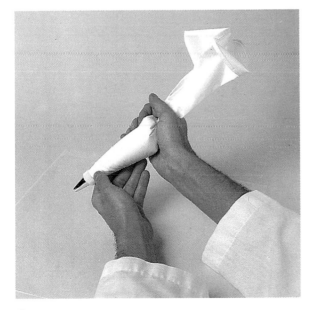

3. This is the proper way to hold the pastry bag.

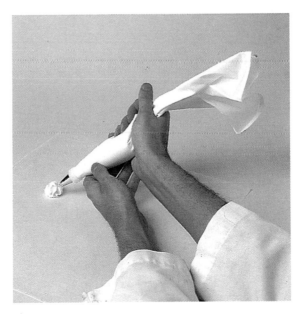

4. After filling the bag and before making any decorations, always "burp" the bag (get rid of any air inside) by squeezing out a little icing.

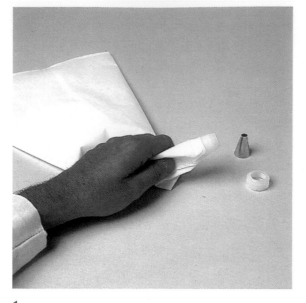

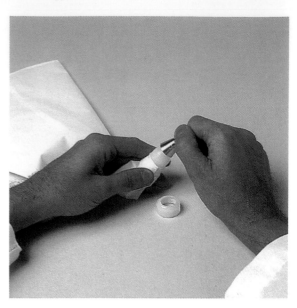

1. Drop the base into the bag so the narrow part clears the opening.

2. Place the tip over the base.

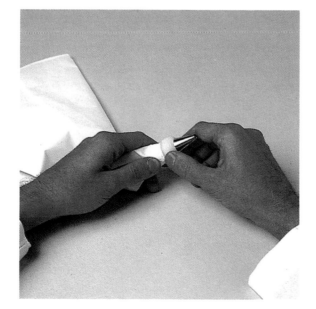

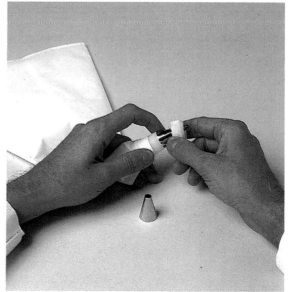

3. Screw the ring onto the threads of the base. This secures the tip to the coupler base.

4. To change tips, simply unscrew the ring, remove the old tip, put on the new one, and screw the ring back on again.

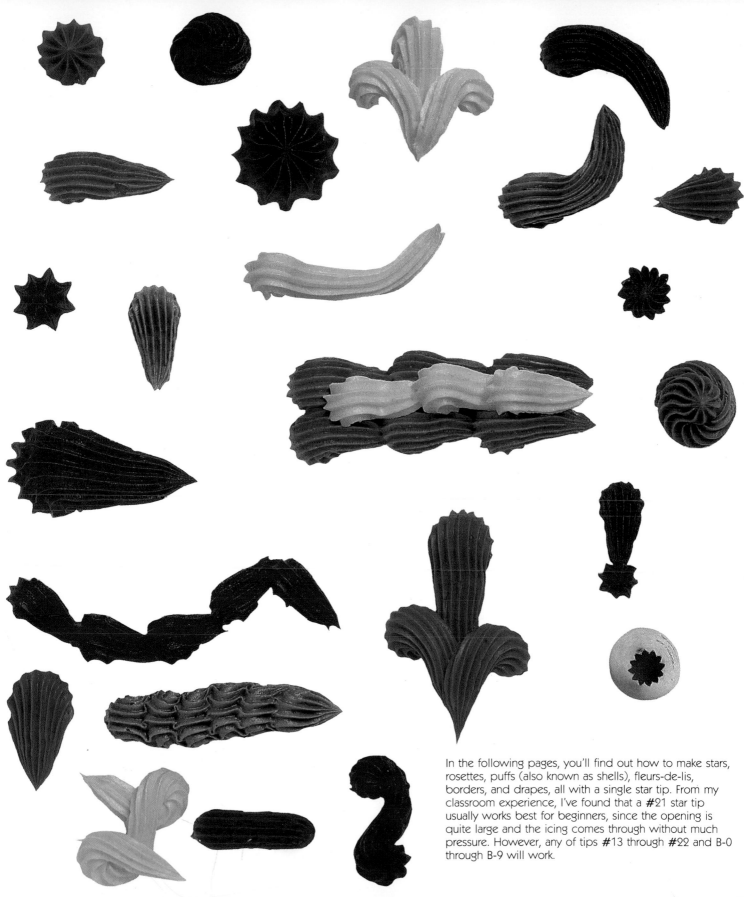

In the following pages, you'll find out how to make stars, rosettes, puffs (also known as shells), fleurs-de-lis, borders, and drapes, all with a single star tip. From my classroom experience, I've found that a #21 star tip usually works best for beginners, since the opening is quite large and the icing comes through without much pressure. However, any of tips #13 through #22 and B-0 through B-9 will work.

Stars

(The quickest and easiest design you can make with a star tip.)

For practice, you'll want to make your designs on a piece of wax or parchment paper. Use a pastry bag fitted with the star tip of your choice and filled with **Butterless Buttercream** icing.

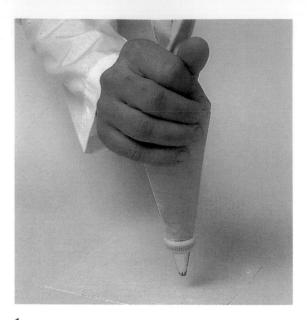

1. Hold your pastry bag vertically, with the tip not quite touching the paper.

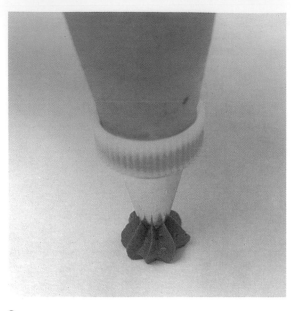

2. Squeeze out a dab of icing.

To turn a star into a simple flower, all you have to do is add a dab of contrasting icing to the center of your star with a #3 (plain) tip.

3. Release pressure and lift.

4. You can make a blanket of stars on your cake by making them close together with one row fitting into the one below it, like bowling pins.

16

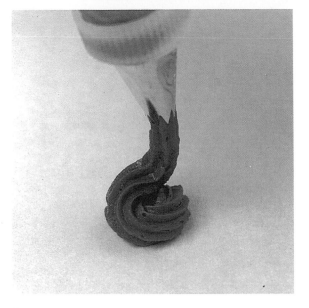

1. Hold your bag vertically, and squeeze out icing while moving your tip slightly to make a small, tight spiral.

2. Release pressure and lift the bag away.

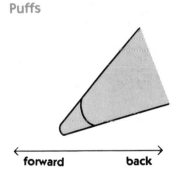

forward ← → back

Moving the bag *back* means moving it *away* from the direction in which the tip is pointing; moving it *forward* means moving it *toward* the direction in which the tip is pointing.

1. Holding your bag at a 45 degree angle, squeeze out a blob of icing as you move the tip slightly forward.

2. Keeping even pressure on the bag, double the icing *back* on itself, and make a tail, releasing the pressure gradually.

Puffs

When you make these buttercream decorations on a cake, always remember to squeeze out a little icing on something that won't matter, like a piece of wax paper. Do this before you start to decorate, and repeat every time you start working again after a break of more than a minute or so. That way, you'll know if there's anything blocking the tip opening (like bits of dried icing) and you can make sure the icing is coming out the way it should be—*before* you make any mistakes on the cake itself.

3. You can also make puffs with short tails.

4. Or with curved tails.

Fleurs-de-lis

(A combination of one long straight puff and two short curved puffs.)

1. Make the long straight puff first.

2. Then make one short curved puff on either side of the long straight one, with all three tails overlapping.

1. To simulate making this border on the edge of a cake, try tracing a semicircle onto the wax or parchment paper.

(A series of overlapping short-tailed puffs.)

2. Follow the curve with a row of overlapping puffs.

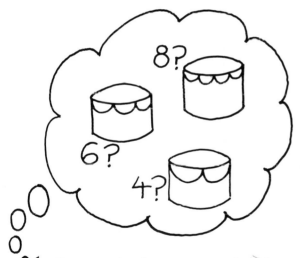

1. First, try to imagine an even number of swags around the side of your cylinder. (The fewer you have, the bigger your swags will be.) Say you want eight. Place the edge of a long spatula down the center of your styrofoam cylinder and make a line along this edge with a pencil. (If you're working on an actual cake, use the edge of the spatula to make a line in the frosting down the center of the cake. You can rub out the lines with a spatula and spray-bottle after you've finished the drapes.)

Drapes

(Swags of overlapping short-tailed puffs that go around the side of a cake.)

The trickiest parts about drapes are getting all the swags the same size and shape, and making the end of the very last swag meet the beginning of the very first one. Experienced cake decorators can get away with eyeballing it, but here's a way for anyone, even a beginner, to get perfect drapes every time.
For practice, work on a cake-like styrofoam cylinder, which you can buy in any five-and-dime.

2. With the same technique, make more lines at even intervals. For 8 swags, you'll be making a total of 4 lines from edge to edge of the cylinder, which will divide its surface into 8 even sections.

3. On the edge of a piece of cardboard, mark the distance between the end points of 2 lines.

4. Place a glass, jar, or bowl on the cardboard so its edge is touching both marks, and trace a semicircle on the cardboard.

5. Cut out the semicircle, and use it to mark swags around the sides of your cylinder. (You'll have to bend the cardboard a little.)

6. Take your pastry bag and run a row of overlapping puffs along one of the swags you just marked.

7. This is how you should start the next swag.

8. Continue in this way around the whole cylinder. The first and last swags should meet perfectly!

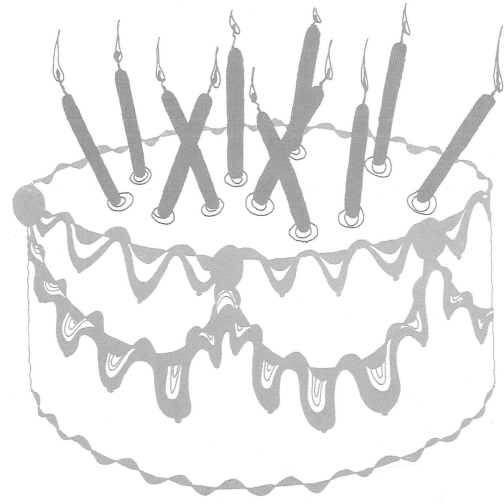

Let's Make a
Chocolate Teddy Bear Cake!

When a friend of a teddy bear is having a birthday, this is the cake to serve. The teddy bear's "fur" is made from lots of double chocolate buttercream icing stars, made with a #21 star tip.

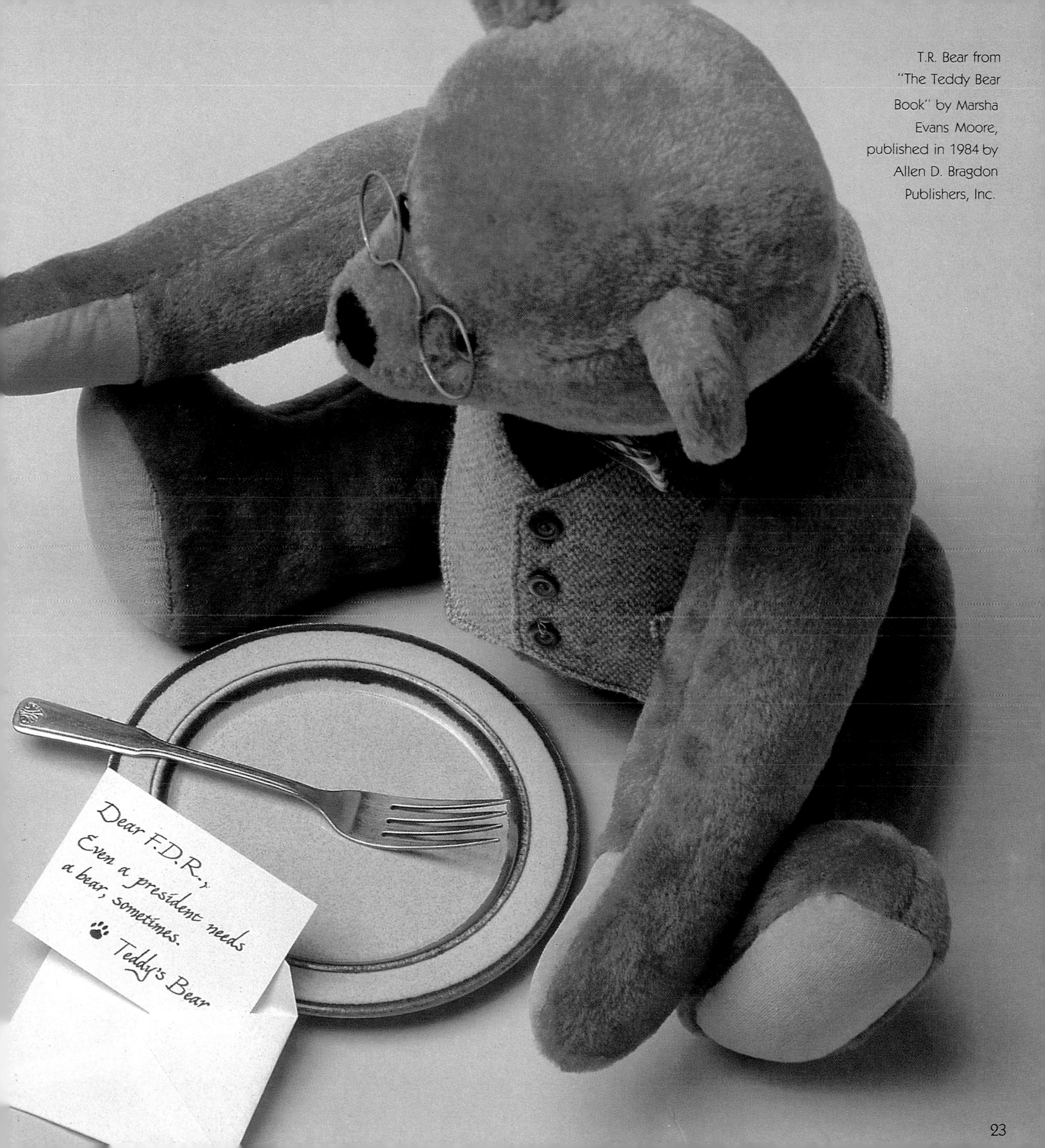

T.R. Bear from
"The Teddy Bear
Book" by Marsha
Evans Moore,
published in 1984 by
Allen D. Bragdon
Publishers, Inc.

Dear F.D.R.,
Even a president needs
a bear, sometimes.
🐾 Teddy's Bear

Dear Mr. Shearson,
I would like to re-submit my
idea for issuing plastic "credit"
cards to use instead of money.
I'm sure it will work.

Master Visa

This super-easy credit card cake gives you just a hint of the magic powers at your disposal, once you've learned a few basic decorating techniques. Eyeball an object, whip up a batch of icing, grab a spatula and a few decorating tips, and Hey Presto! You've turned a plain cake into a creation everyone will oooh and aaah over. Who would have guessed that something so banal as plastic money could inspire such creativity?

Let's Make a
Credit Cake!

AMERICAN EXPRESS

[3712 345678 95006]

HAPPY BIRTHDAY LARRY

Chocolate Teddy Bear Cake

I made my teddy bear with a delicious chocolate and honey-flavored cake. It's the very favorite of T.R., the bear in the picture who's patiently waiting for a slice. Here's the recipe:

Chocolate-Honey Cake

8 ounces melted semi-sweet chocolate
1 ⅓ cups honey
3 ½ cups sifted cake flour
2 teaspoons baking soda
1 ½ teaspoons salt
1 cup room-temperature butter
1 cup sugar
1 ½ cups water
2 teaspoons vanilla extract
4 eggs

Melt chocolate in a double boiler. Add honey. Sift flour once, measure, add baking soda and salt; sift together 2 times. In the bowl of an electric mixer cream butter and sugar until light and fluffy. Add chocolate-honey mixture, water, and vanilla. Mix. Add eggs, one at a time, beating thoroughly after each addition. Add flour gradually. Grease an 8" × 3" cake pan and 3 cupcake tins. Fill pans half-way. Bake 1 ½ hours at 325 degrees. Extra batter can be used for extra cupcakes.

You'll also need a double batch of buttercream icing (recipe of your choice from the beginning of this chapter). Set aside about 2 tablespoons of the icing, which you'll leave white. Color ¼ cup of the icing with a little red food color to turn it pink. To ⅔ of the balance, add ¼ cup melted unsweetened chocolate. To the rest, add ¼ cup unsweetened Dutch-process cocoa plus 2 tablespoons water.

Assemble the round cake and the cupcakes as indicated in the diagram. Using a #21 star tip, cover all but the ears of the teddy bear with dark double chocolate buttercream stars. With the same tip, cover the teddy bear's ears with chocolate buttercream and pink buttercream. Make the white part of the teddy bear's eyes with white buttercream and the same #21 tip. (Hold the pastry bag vertically, and squeeze out more icing than you would for a star.) Use chocolate buttercream and a #3 (plain) tip for the dark part of the teddy bear's eyes and for his nose and mouth.

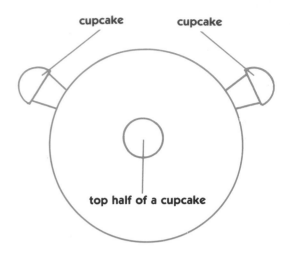

cupcake   cupcake

top half of a cupcake

Cut the bottom half off a cupcake and place the top half in the middle of the 8" cake to form a mound for the teddy bear's nose.

Lay 2 cupcakes on their sides against the 8" cake for the teddy bear's ears.

Credit Cake

Here's a perfect illustration of how easy it is to put together an original, imaginative cake with a minimum of fuss and effort. This Credit Cake is made out of 2 13" × 9" × 2" sheet cakes, to make a 13" × 9" credit card that's 4" thick, and frosted with buttercream icing colored with 4 parts blue, 6 parts green, and 1 part yellow food color. The white border is a simple line of white buttercream piped through a #21 (star) tip. The black inner border is made of a series of black buttercream stars, and a small fleur-de-lis in each corner, piped through a #16 tip. The logo in the middle is a dab of white buttercream spread into a disk with a spatula, bordered by a white buttercream line piped through a #3 (plain round) tip; the lines of the face are piped through a #3 tip. All the writing is done with a #3 tip. (For tips on writing with icing, look ahead to the royal icing chapter.)

1. Using a pastry bag fitted with any large tip, pipe icing randomly onto the top and sides of your cake.
(You can transfer the cake to a turntable either before or after this step.)

2. Use a spatula to spread the icing evenly over the surface of the cake, while spraying liberally with water from a mister. (For more information on this technique, see the "Tools of the Trade" section in the appendix.) Continue smoothing and spraying until the icing is perfectly even.

Texturing the Cake With Paper Towels

You can use this simple technique to create a textured surface on your frosted cake. The texture varies with the brand of paper towel you choose.

1. Lay 3 layers of paper towels onto the frosted cake, and use a mister to spray the paper towels with water.

2. Spray the cake as you lift the paper towels off (the water helps unstick the paper from the icing). Use the same technique for the sides of the cake.

Chapter 2

ROYAL: THE ARISTOCRAT OF ICING

From the cake decorator's point of view, the single most important difference between royal and buttercream icings is that royal dries hard. This allows you to mass-produce as many decorations as you want, and save them until you need to use them. Royal has other advantages, especially for beginners. You can make all your royal icing decorations off the cake, on a piece of wax or parchment paper, so you don't have to worry about making a mistake on your cake. Also, you can throw away all the decorations you don't think turned out so well and save only the very best ones.

Dear Louis,
Let 'em eat cake.
Marie

This crown cake is made with 2 8" cakes, candy dough, and royal icing. See the next page for instructions.

Underneath all the ornate glitter of this crown cake are 2 8" round cakes, the edges of the top one bevelled to create a dome. It's frosted with white and deep purple royal icing. The gold structures on top are made of candy dough (recipe in the candy dough chapter) rolled out and cut into strips, Maltese crosses, and fleurs-de-lis, with a hand-formed ball of candy dough beneath the top cross. The candy dough pieces are painted with egg white and sprinkled with gold edible glitter. Silver dragees and hard candy "jewels" are embedded in ochre royal icing piped onto the candy dough pieces (ochre is a mixture of yellow and brown).

Since royal icing will dry out if exposed to the air, you must keep any icing you're not using in an airtight container with a piece of dampened cheesecloth under the lid. Take icing from the container as you need it. Also, you'll need to use your tip stick periodically to clean out bits of dried icing in your tip opening. If you have to leave your bag for a few minutes, or if you need to switch to another bag for a moment, be sure to cover the tip of the bag with a tip cap, and to fold the end of the pastry bag as tight as you can.

From the point of view of the person eating your cake, the biggest differences between royal and buttercream icings are flavor and consistency: royal icing has no shortening, and lacks the creamy taste and texture of buttercream. So remember that, as far as your tongue is concerned, royal icing decorations are nothing more than crunchy sugar and, like sugar cubes, are enjoyable only in moderation. I do find, though, that the crunchy texture of royal decorations can contrast nicely with the smoothness of buttercream. If you use royal icing decorations on a cake frosted with buttercream (or another smooth and creamy icing), you can have a visually stunning cake that you'll love to eat, too!

Here are three royal icing recipes, one with egg whites and two with meringue powder (which is basically dried egg whites). I prefer meringue powder to egg whites, since royal icing made with egg whites can't be re-mixed to its proper consistency. Also, meringue powder is cheaper than real eggs, and is just as good taste-wise. (See the appendix to find out where to buy meringue powder). Royal icing has a shelf life of one to two weeks if kept in an airtight container with a piece of damp cheesecloth.

Basic Royal Icing

6 tablespoons water
3 tablespoons meringue powder
4 cups confectioners sugar, sifted
Measure meringue powder and water into a bowl, and beat at high speed with an electric mixer for 30 seconds. Add sifted confectioners sugar. Mix at low speed for 1 minute, and at high speed for 7 to 8 minutes until icing is stiff, but not dry. If you draw a knife or spatula through it, the path should be clear and hold its shape.

Basic Royal Icing: Large Batch

½ cup plus 2 tablespoons water
6 tablespoons meringue powder
8 cups confectioners sugar, sifted
Measure meringue powder and water into a large bowl and beat at high speed with an electric mixer for 30 seconds. Add sifted confectioners sugar. Beat for 2 minutes at low speed, and for 5 to 7 minutes at high speed. A knife or spatula drawn through the icing should leave a clear path that doesn't collapse.

After these icings have been stored for more than an hour or so, they should be re-beaten to regain this same consistency.

Egg White Royal Icing

3 large or extra large egg whites
3 teaspoons cream of tartar
4 cups confectioners sugar, sifted
Measure all the ingredients into a bowl. With an electric mixer, beat for 2 minutes at low speed and 8 to 10 minutes at high speed. A knife or spatula drawn through the icing should leave a clear path that holds its shape.

Coloring Your Icing

It's best to color royal icing with paste or powder color. If you use liquid color, it must be absolutely oil-free. For more information on colors and coloring agents, see the "Colors and Coloring Techniques" section in the appendix.

In the pages that follow, you'll learn how to make this garden of drop flowers, leaves, and rosebuds. (They can also be made in buttercream with the same techniques I describe here—but, of course, they can't be stored and they must be made directly on the cake.)

You will need:
Wax or parchment paper
Pastry bag filled with royal icing
  the color you want your drop
  flowers to be and fitted with a
  drop flower tip (I used #223)
Pastry bag filled with royal icing
  the color you want your flower
  center to be (probably yellow
  or, if the other bag has yellow
  in it, green), fitted with a #3
  (plain) tip

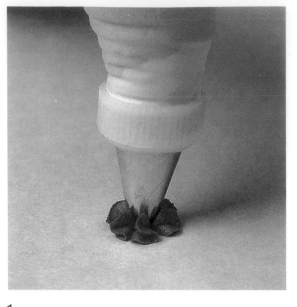

1. First, you'll need the bag with the drop flower tip. Holding the bag vertically, touch the tip opening to the wax or parchment paper, and squeeze out a blob of icing.

2. Release pressure and lift.

The drop flower tip is designed to produce a nearly-complete flower with one squeeze of the pastry bag; all that has to be added to finish the flower is a single dot in the center with a plain tip.

To make a flower with swirled petals, use the same materials and technique as for the straight drop flower, *except:* Cock your wrist and twist the bag as you squeeze out the flower.

3. Now, you'll need the bag with the plain tip. Place a dab of icing in the center of your flower.

4. That's all there is to making a drop flower. You can turn out dozens in no time.

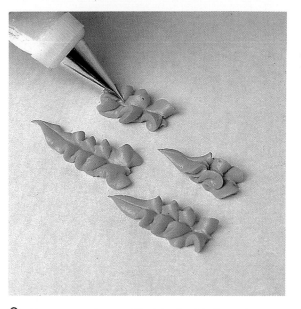

You will need:
Wax or parchment paper
Pastry bag filled with green royal
   icing and fitted with a leaf tip
   (I used #349 for the plain leaf,
   and #352 for the ruffled and
   vertical leaves)

1. Holding the bag at a 45 degree angle, squeeze out a dab of icing, release pressure, and pull the bag quickly back to pull the leaf to a tip.

2. You can make a ruffled leaf with the same technique, *except*: double the icing back on itself as you move the bag.

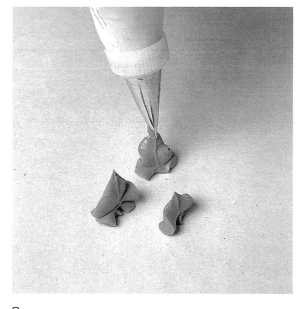

Since royal icing dries quickly, try this trick: keep a glass of warm water handy, and dip the tip into the water every once in a while. The water will dissolve any dried bits of icing that may clog your tip opening.

3. Or, you can make standing leaves by holding the bag vertically and moving the bag straight up as you squeeze.

4. You can get different sizes, all with a single tip, just by varying the pressure on the bag.

Rosebuds

Rosebuds are a little more challenging than drop flowers and leaves, but with a little practice, you'll be turning them out like hotcakes.

You will need:
Wax or parchment paper
Pastry bag filled with royal icing the color you want your rosebuds to be and fitted with a #104 (rose) tip
Pastry bag filled with green royal icing and fitted with a #3 (plain) tip

The first 2 pictures show how the rosebud looks from the perspective of someone standing in *front* of the person making the bud; the pictures of the stem and sepals are from the perspective of the person making them.

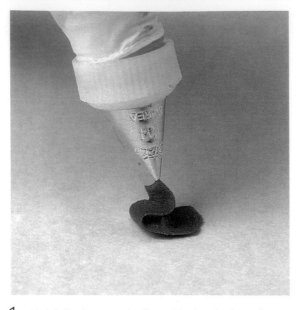 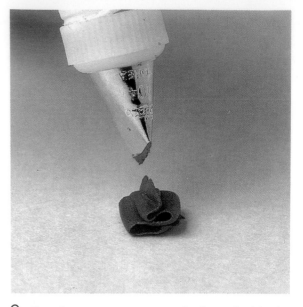

1. Hold the bag vertically, with the tip just above the paper, and with the fat end of the tip opening towards you. Squeeze out a band of icing while moving the tip about ½ an inch sideways. Keeping even pressure on the bag, double the band of icing *back* on itself.

2. Keeping even pressure on the bag, double the band of icing back again, and halfway back again. Release pressure and lift the bag away.

Stem and Sepals

If you're making lots of rosebuds for future use, I suggest making the bud first, and adding the sepals and stem only after the bud has been placed on the cake. The stem is too thin and delicate to be stored safely, and if you leave the sepals until the very end as well, you'll be sure to match greens.

1. To make the stem and sepals, you'll need the bag with the green icing and the plain tip. Holding your bag at a 45 degree angle, make a U along the bottom edge of your rosebud.

2. Turn the U into a W.

3. Continue this center line as a zigzag at the very base of the rosebud, and straighten out again to make the stem.

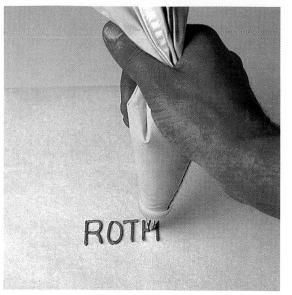

1. When making printed letters, hold the bag vertically.

You will need:
Wax or parchment paper
Pastry bag filled with royal icing and fitted with a #1, #2, or #3 plain round tip

For practice, you'll want to write on wax or parchment paper. Remember to always hold the tip a little above, not touching, the writing surface. Once you're good at writing in icing, you can write directly on your cake.

The same techniques you learn for writing with royal icing apply to writing with other kinds of icing.

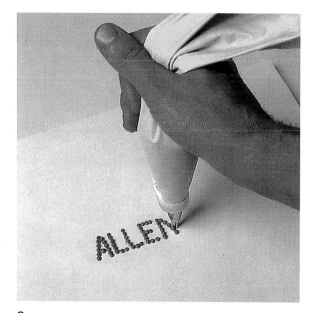

2. Hold the bag the same way for printed letter made with a series of dots.

3. For script, slant the bag a little as you write.

Piping gel is a transparent, gelatinous substance ideal for writing messages on a cake. It comes ready-mixed from the store in a variety of colors. If you want, you can add paste, powder, or liquid color to achieve a special tint.
Fill your pastry bag with piping gel the same way you fill it with any other icing. I recommend a #1, #2, or #3 tip for writing. Piping gel is uniformly smooth and will come out of the bag evenly with little pressure. If you need to have a stiffer consistency for better control, put the gel in the refrigerator or freezer for a few minutes. Always leave writing a message with piping gel until just before you serve the cake; otherwise, the gel will bleed into the icing beneath it.
Keep piping gel in an airtight container and refrigerate it at all times when not in use.

Let's Make a
Candy Cottage!

"...Suddenly they came into a cleared place in the forest and saw a cottage with a steep roof that reached almost to the ground. When they went close up to it, they saw that the cottage was made of bread and cakes, and the window panes were of clear sugar..."

All you need to make a candy cottage every bit as enchanting as the one Hansel and Gretel stumbled upon is a batch of gingerbread dough, some royal icing, and a few assorted goodies.

Gingerbread Dough

12 cups flour	1 ½ cups honey
12 tablespoons baking powder	3 ½ cups sugar
2 tablespoons ground cinnamon	½ cup butter
2 teaspoons ground cloves	Juice and grated peel of 1 lemon
2 teaspoons ground ginger	2 extra large eggs
½ teaspoon ground cardamom	2 extra large egg yolks
¼ teaspoon salt	

Side (cut 2)

In a large bowl, combine flour, baking powder, cinnamon, cloves, ginger, cardamom, and salt.

In a 4- or 5-quart saucepan, bring honey, sugar, and butter to a boil over high heat, stirring with a large wooden spoon until sugar is dissolved and butter is melted. Remove from heat and stir in lemon juice and peel. Cool to room temperature.

When cool, beat in 6 cups of flour mixture until well blended. Beat in eggs and egg yolks, and then beat in remaining flour mixture.

Flour hands and knead dough until it is smooth and pliable but still slightly sticky. If too moist to handle, beat in more flour 1 tablespoon at a time.

Cutting and Baking:

Make cardboard templates from the patterns provided. (Follow the instructions for making templates at the beginning of the cookies chapter.) Cut out 2 roof templates (1 for each roof piece), a template for the back without window and door cut out, a template for the front with window and door cut out, and a template for *each* side piece. The reason you make a cardboard template for *every* piece is that you'll use them as a permanent backing to support the cottage walls and roof.

Roll out the dough to a thickness of about ¼" on 2 well-greased cookie sheets.

Lay lightly floured templates on the dough and cut around the outlines with a sharp knife. Then cut out door and window openings, but save pieces to reattach to openings later. Paint a corn syrup-water mixture (3 parts corn syrup to 1 part water) onto the cut-out pieces to make them shiny.

Bake pieces at 350 degrees 10 to 12 minutes. Poke dough occasionally to let air escape. After baking, remove to a rack and let cool.

Assembling and Decorating:

While the front piece and the roof pieces are lying flat, make the following decorations on them: Attach the shutters with dabs of royal icing, and use royal icing to affix a candied orange slice to each shutter. Use a #14 (small star) tip to make star borders around the window and the door frame. Attach a piece of sesame candy for the flower box. Make royal icing drop flowers with a #218 tip, and leaves with a #349 tip. The little fir trees against the front of the cottage are made by piping strips of royal icing through a #14 (star) tip over 2 mounds of royal icing. Frost the roof pieces with royal icing, and embed candy in the icing. Add stars of royal icing between the pieces of candy with a #18 tip.

Pipe royal icing onto cardboard templates for walls and roof and attach to the backs of the pieces. Let dry completely (about 4 hours) before assembling pieces.

Cut out a stiff base of heavy cardboard about 12" × 10".

Pipe icing on bottom edges of 1 side wall, position in place, and hold in place until set, about 5 minutes.

Apply icing to edge of side wall adjoining back and to bottom edge of back wall. Place back wall in position, and hold until set.

Position other side and front in same way. If you need to prop the pieces, place unopened food cans against the walls. Allow structure to dry completely.

Pipe icing along slanted edges of front and back walls and put 1 roof piece in postion. Prop with a food can, using folded paper towels as a cushion between the can and the gingerbread. Let dry completely, then repeat for the other roof piece.

Place door in position, using royal icing to hold it in place.

Use a #18 (star) tip to make decorative star borders along the corners and roof edges of the cottage.

To make the broom, use a cinnamon stick and royal icing piped through a #3 (plain round) tip.

The toad stools are made with a #12 (large plain round) tip, and a #3 tip is used for the dots on top.

Roof (cut 2)

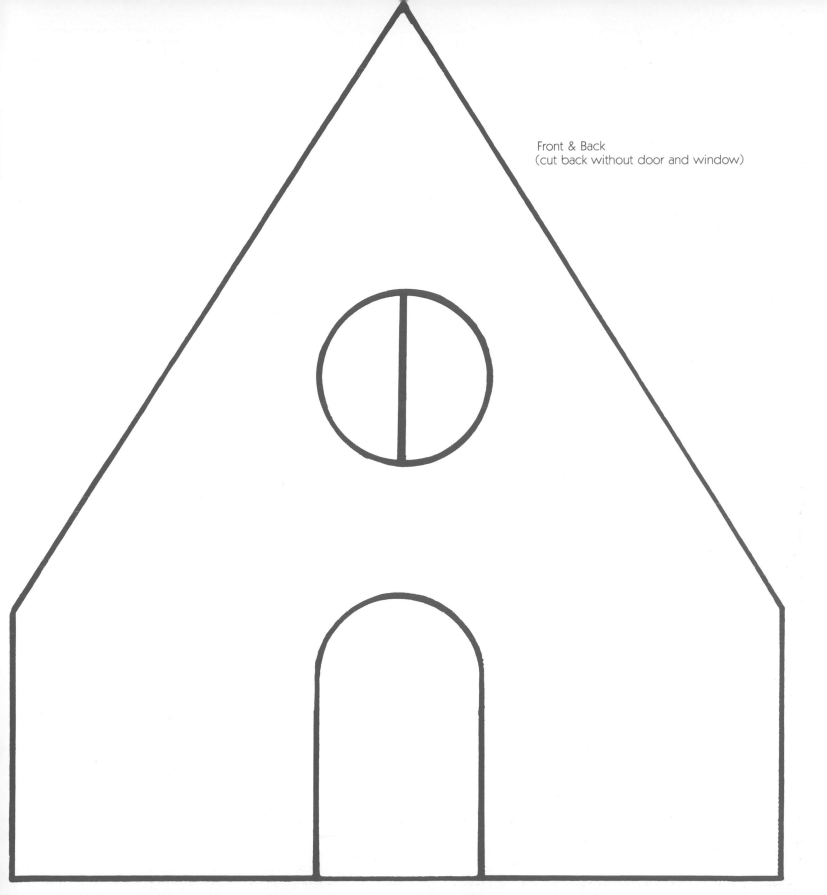

Front & Back
(cut back without door and window)

CREATIVE

COOKIES

Chapter 3

You can use store-bought cookie cutters or a small, sharp knife to make cookies like the ones pictured. If you want to reproduce any of the cookies you see in this chapter, look at the how-to instructions for making templates.

The thin lines on the cookies pictures are made with royal icing piped through a #2 tip. The solid blocks of color are made with flow frosting, which is royal icing thinned with water. To make flow frosting, mix up a batch of royal icing (follow one of the recipes at the beginning of the royal icing chapter). Add water, a little bit at a time, until the icing flows slowly in an even stream, like heavy cream. Color flow frosting the same way you color royal icing.

There are a number of ways you can apply flow frosting to your cookies. You can pipe a little onto the cookie with a pastry bag, and then spread it out onto the area you want to cover with a spatula, knife, spoon, or toothpick. Or, you can use a spoon or spatula to get the flow frosting onto the cookie, and then spread it out the same way. Some people like to use an artist's brush to paint flow frosting onto the cookie. Once you've decorated your cookies, let them sit someplace out of the way until the flow frosting is dry. Flow frosting dries hard the same way royal icing does. If you want to use dragees, nonpareils, or confetti to embellish your cookies, place them in the flow frosting before it's had a chance to dry.

You'll notice that some of the cookies, like the watermelon slice, the tulip, and the strawberries, are shinier than the others. They're decorated with egg yolk glaze instead of flow frosting. To make the glaze, mix 1 egg yolk with ¼ teaspoon water. If you want several colors of glaze, separate the egg yolk-water mixture into several small containers, and color as desired. Paint the designs on your cookies *before* baking them.

The cookies pictured are made with 3 kinds of cookie dough. The light- colored ones are sugar cookies, and the darker ones are gingerbread and spice cookies. Here are the recipes:

Spice Cookies

2 ¼ cups sifted flour
1 teaspoon baking soda
1 tablespoon ground cinnamon
1 ½ teaspoons ground cloves
½ teaspoon ground cardamom
¼ teaspoon ground ginger
¾ cups room temperature butter
¾ cup light brown sugar
3 tablespoons warm water
2 tablespoons molasses

Sift the flour, baking soda, cinnamon, cloves, cardamom, and ginger together. Cream the butter and sugar in a separate bowl. Mix in water and molasses. Mix in dry ingredients, a little bit at a time. Ball up the dough, wrap it in wax paper, and refrigerate 2 to 4 hours.

Roll out the dough on a floured surface to a thickness of about ¼" and cut out the shapes.

Place on a greased cookie sheet and bake at 350 degrees for 8 to 10 minutes or until the cookies are slightly dark around the edges.

This recipe makes enough dough for about 3 dozen cookies.

Sugar Cookies

½ cup room temperature butter
1 cup sugar
1 egg
1 tablespoon cream
1 teaspoon vanilla
2 cups sifted flour
¼ teaspoon salt
1 teaspoon baking powder

Cream butter and add sugar gradually. Beat until fluffy. Add the remaining wet ingredients, beating well as you add. Sift dry ingredients together and add to the butter mixture. Mix well. Refrigerate 3 hours.

Roll out the dough on a floured surface to a thickness of about ⅛", and cut out shapes.

Place on a greased baking sheet and bake at 375 degrees for about 7 minutes.

This recipe makes enough dough for about 3 dozen cookies.

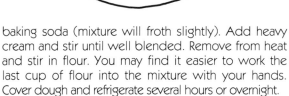

Gingerbread Cookies

8 ounces margarine or butter
3 cups sugar
1 cup molasses
3 tablespoons ginger
1 tablespoon cloves
1 egg
2 tablespoons baking soda
1 cup heavy cream
9 cups flour

Melt the margarine in a large stainless steel saucepan, then add the sugar, molasses, and spices. Stir over low heat until well blended. Stir in the egg and the baking soda (mixture will froth slightly). Add heavy cream and stir until well blended. Remove from heat and stir in flour. You may find it easier to work the last cup of flour into the mixture with your hands. Cover dough and refrigerate several hours or overnight.

Roll out the dough on a floured surface to a thickness of about ⅛" and cut out the shapes.

Place on a greased cookie sheet and bake at 350 degrees for 5 minutes.

This recipe makes enough dough for about 12 dozen cookies.

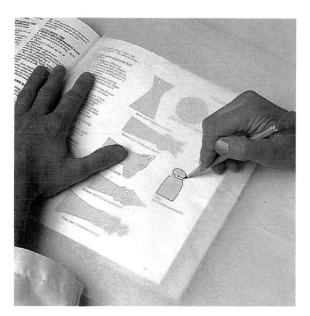

1. Place tracing paper (or any paper you can see through) over the pattern printed on the page of the book. Use a pencil to draw the outline of the pattern on the tracing paper.

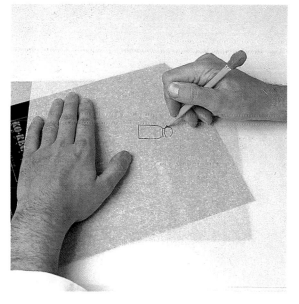

2. Lay a piece of cardboard on a flat surface, and place a piece of carbon paper, shiny side down, on the cardboard. Lay the tracing paper with the pattern outline on top of the carbon paper. Retrace the outline with your pencil; this will transfer the outline to the piece of cardboard. Use a sharp scissors to cut out the cardboard template.

Using Patterns to Make Cardboard or Paper Templates

You can use this technique to make templates from any of the patterns in this book. To make a cookie pictured in this chapter, treat the cookie pictured as a pattern, and lay the tracing paper directly over the cookie and trace its outline. When you've made your template, you can lay it on some rolled-out cookie dough and cut along the edges of the template, thus cutting out a piece of dough the same shape as the cookie you traced from the book.

Farmyard Cookies

44

Political Party Cookies

au revoir

46

Cookies of Love & Affection

I Love You

Welcome Home

for my Teacher

Mother

Cookies for a Summertime Picnic

Easter Cookies

Birthday Party Cookies

49

Chapter 4 CHARACTER CAKES

The bodies, arms, and legs of these clowns, and the puff border around the bottom edge of the cake, are made with a 4-B (star) tip. The smaller puff border around the top edge of the cake is made with a #21 star tip. The ruffles around the clowns' wrists and ankles are made with a #68 (leaf) tip. The feet, hands, and buttons are made with a #8 (plain round) tip. You can buy clown heads like the ones pictured at cake decorating or doll supply stores.

Dear P.T.,
Meet you by
the elephants.
Bailey

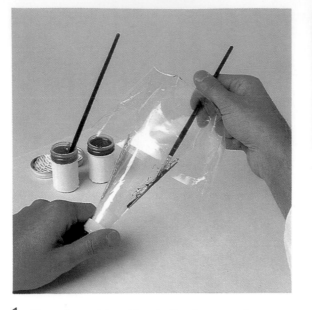

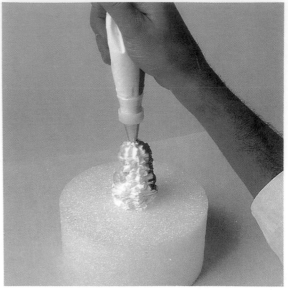

1. To make a striped body like the ones the clowns on my clown cake have, stripe paste color directly onto the inside of a disposable bag with a brush or spatula. Fill the bag as usual with buttercream or royal icing. I'm using a #21 star tip for the clown in the pictures.

2. The first part of the clown you make is the body. Squeeze out a thick blob of icing.

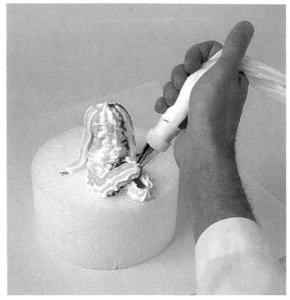

3. Next, make the arms.

4. Next, make the legs. The arms and the legs can be in any position you want. You can make them spread apart, close together, or crossed.

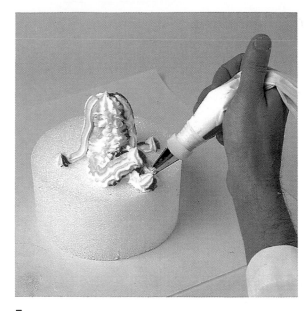

5. Next make, the feet and hands with a simple star (you can also make the feet and hands with a blob or dab of icing from a plain tip).

6. Make the ruffles around the ankles and wrists with a leaf tip. In the picture, I'm using a #349 tip.

7. Add the head and any final decorations. In the picture, I'm using red hots for buttons.

8. If you want a reclining clown, just push him over.

Character Heads

It's not hard to turn simple, inexpensive store-bought character heads into fun and playful additions to a cake. In this chapter, I show you how to use icing to merge a plastic head into a body that can sit up, lie down, or assume any postion you want it to.

Chapter 5
ROWS & ROWS
OF ROSES

In this chapter, I'll show you how to make professional-looking flowers on a "nail" and on wire. The techniques you'll learn are a step up from the ones I've shown you so far, because you'll be manipulating the pastry bag in one hand and the nail or wire in the other. With a little practice, though, you'll soon be turning out flawless flowers by the dozen.

Forming a Perfect Rose on a "Nail"

You will need:

Size 7, 9, or 13 flower nail

Several squares of wax or parchment paper, each one a little larger than the head of the nail you're using (about 2" × 2")

Pastry bag filled with either royal or buttercream icing in the color you want your roses to be **Remember that if you use royal icing, you'll be able to make as many roses as you want and save them a long time.**

#12 (plain round) and a 104 (rose) tip (if you're not using bags that accomodate couplers, you must use two pastry bags, each equipped with one of these tips)

Piece of styrofoam (to stick your nail into in case you want to pause or take a rest while making your rose)

1. In your left hand, hold the nail between thumb and fingers so you can twirl it easily. If you're left-handed, hold the nail in your right hand.

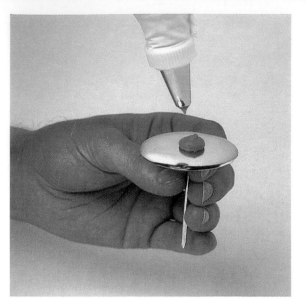

2. The first tip you'll need is the *#12*. Place a dab of icing on the center of your nail.

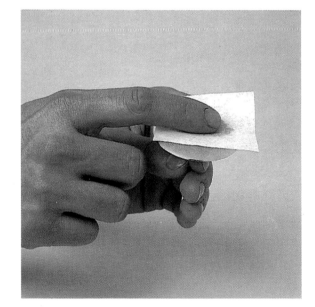

3. Press a square of parchment paper onto the dab.

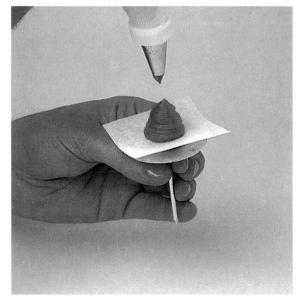

4. Holding the bag vertically a little above the center of the nail, squeeze out the beehive-shaped *base* of your rose. When the beehive of icing is a little higher than it is wide at the bottom, release the pressure completely and lift the bag away.

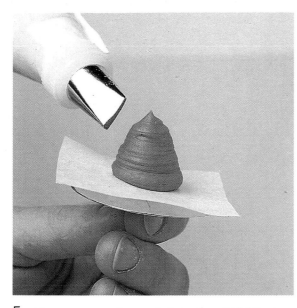

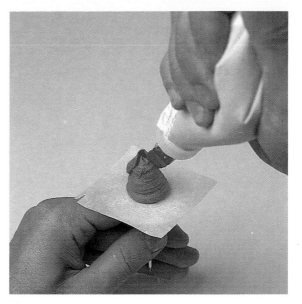

When I'm showing my students how to make a rose on a nail, I always tell them to come around behind me and look over my shoulder to see how I do it. That way, they see it from the perspective of the person who's making the rose. That's why I told the photographer to come around behind me and point the camera over my shoulder for the next pictures.

5. Now, you need to switch to the *#104* tip to make the rose petals. The *skinny top end* of the tip opening should be facing *up* and turned about 45 degrees to the left. If you're left-handed, you'll be holding the pastry bag in your left hand, and the tip opening will be tilted to the right.

6. Touch the bottom (fat) end of the tip opening to a point about halfway down the base, and squeeze out a ribbon of icing while turning the nail in a counterclockwise direction. If you're left-handed, turn it in a clockwise direction.

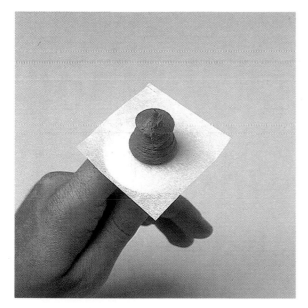

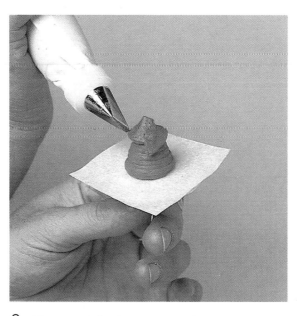

Now, you'll be coming in front of me again to see how to angle the tip opening (step 8), and then coming back behind me to watch steps 9 on.

7. With the bottom of the end of the tip once again touching the base, release the pressure on the bag and break off the ribbon after you have made one full turn of the nail. The 2 ends of the ribbon should overlap slightly.

8. Now, to make the open petals, you must turn the top skinny end of the tip opening 45 degrees to the *right* (to the left if you're left-handed). The tilt of the pastry bag should not be quite as steep as when you made the first petal.

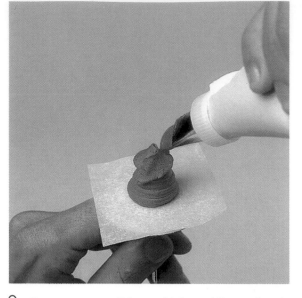

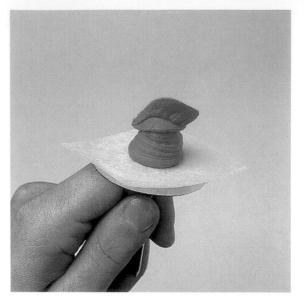

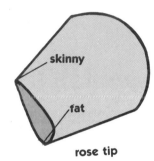

skinny

fat

rose tip

9. Squeeze out a ribbon of icing while turning the nail in a counterclockwise direction (clockwise if you're left-handed). This time, though, don't turn it a full revolution, but stop after you've made about ⅓ of a complete turn. Also, move the tip up a little as you reach the middle of your turn and lower it again as you approach the end.

10. This is how your petal should look up close from the side. Note how it goes up in the middle and then down again at the end. This helps make the rose look full instead of flat.

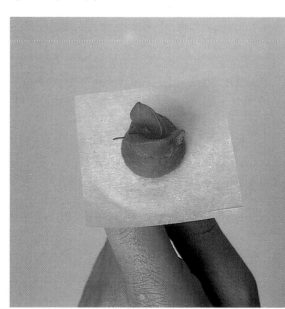

11. Start the next petal about halfway along the curve of the last one, so they overlap. Use the same up-and-down motion of the tip while squeezing the bag and rotating the nail.

12. Continue down the base in this way, starting each new petal halfway along the curve of the last one, so they overlap. Use the same up-and-down motion of the tip. Also, make the bag and tip angles a little flatter with each petal, so that the petals look more and more open the farther down the base you go.

13. This is what the completed rose looks like.

14. If you're working with buttercream, you can use scissors to cut the rose from the nail and place it directly on your cake. If the cake isn't ready, you can lift the parchment paper off the nail and put the rose in the freezer. This will make it easier to handle when you want to put it on your cake.

If you're working with royal icing, the parchment paper may be removed from the nail and placed on a cookie sheet for 24 hours for the rose to dry. Once you've removed the rose from the nail, you can use the same nail to make more roses.

Variation: Making a Rose on a Toothpick or Short Piece of Flower Wire

Using essentially the same technique you used to make your rose on a nail, you can make smaller roses permanently mounted on a toothpick or short piece of flower wire.

You will need:
Several toothpicks or short pieces of cloth-coated 12 gauge flower wire

Pastry bag fitted with a #3 (plain) tip and filled with royal icing the color you want your rose to be; you'll also need a #101 (rose) tip for that same bag of icing—or, if you don't have a bag that accomodates a coupler, you'll need a second bag fitted with a #101 tip and filled with royal icing the color you want your rose to be

Pastry bag fitted with a #349 (leaf) tip and filled with green icing

Block of styrofoam

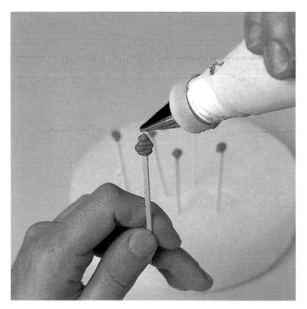

1. Using the pastry bag with the **#3** tip, make a coil of icing at the top of your toothpick or wire. This is the base of your rose. Stick the toothpick or wire into the styrofoam, and leave one hour for the icing to dry. Remember to close the end of your pastry bag tight and to put a tip cap over the tip.

2. Now, switch to the bag with the **#101** tip, and follow the instructions for making the petals of the rose on a nail (steps 5-13). Then, make 4 or 5 leaves beneath the rose with the **#349** tip (you can refer to the "Leaves" section of the royal icing chapter if you need to).

Dear F.T.D.,
But I distinctly said
flowers by wire.
Marconi

Flowers on Wire

You can create a stunning effect by grouping your flowers on wire in a spray on top of your cake. They can also be bent slightly without cracking the icing, and used in a decorative motif around the sides of a cake, or wrapped around the columns of a tiered wedding cake.

Method #1

You will need:
Several pieces of cloth-coated
  12- gauge flower wire
3 pastry bags:
1 with a #3 (plain round) tip
  and royal icing the color you
  want your flower center to be
1 with a #101 (rose) or #101 S
  (small rose) tip and royal icing
  the color you want your flower
  petals to be
1 with a #349 (leaf) tip and
  green royal icing
Block of styrofoam

Flowers on wire are quick and
easy to make, and will keep a
long time in a covered
container. They must dry hard
to be storeable, so they can
only be made with royal icing.

These pictures are all from the
perspective of the person
making the flowers on wire.

Left-handers:

In step 3, you should tilt the
skinny end of the tip opening
up and to the *right,* you
should touch it to the *right*
side of the flower base, and
you should turn the wire in a
counterclockwise direction.

Technically, the "leaves" in step
4 are actually *sepals,* which are
modified leaves just below
the petals of a flower.

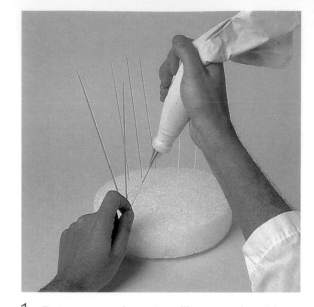

1. To turn your wire a stem-like green, insert it through the opening of the #349 tip on the bag with green icing, and withdraw it slowly while squeezing lightly on the bag. Coat all your wires in this manner, sticking them into the styrofoam as you go. Give them a few minutes to dry.

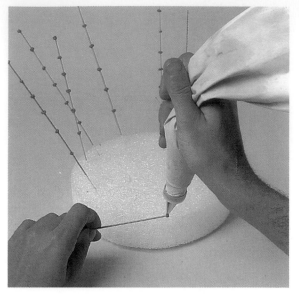

2. Now, change to the bag with the #3 tip. Holding your wire horizontally and your bag vertically above the wire, squeeze out a line of icing while turning the wire so that you have a small "doughnut" of icing on the wire; this is the flower center. Repeat at even intervals along the wires. Allow to dry 10 minutes.

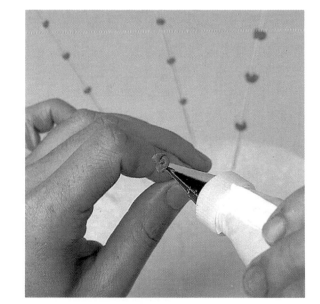

3. Now, change to the bag with the #101 or #101 S tip. Tilt the skinny end of the tip opening up and to the left, touching it to the left side of the flower center. Use an up-and- down motion of the tip as you squeeze out icing and turn the wire in a clockwise direction. Make about 6 petals on each flower center.

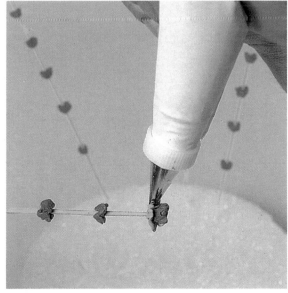

4. Now, change to the bag with the #349 (leaf) tip and the green icing. Holding the wire more or less horizontally, place the tip against a point just beneath one of the flowers, and squeeze out a leaf, using the technique described in the "Leaves" section of the royal icing chapter. Make 3 to 5 beneath each flower.

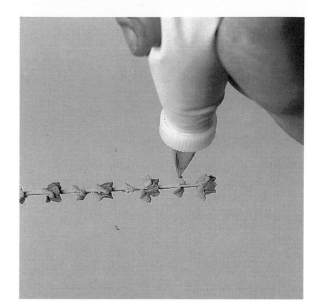

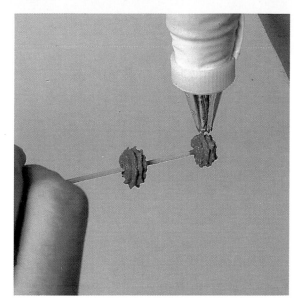

Method #2: One-step Technique for Simple Flowers on Wire

You will need:
Several pieces of cloth-coated
   12-gauge flower wire
Pastry bag equipped with a star
   tip (I used #18) and filled with
   royal icing the color you want
   your flowers to be
Pastry bag fitted with any plain
   round tip and filled with green
   royal icing
Block of styrofoam

5. To make true leaves, repeat the technique for making sepals, except place the tip about midway between two flowers instead of immediately beneath each one.

Coat your wires in the green icing using the technique described under Method #1. Then, take the pastry bag fitted with the star tip and make little "star doughnuts" at even intervals along the wire, just like you did when making the flower centers under Method #1.

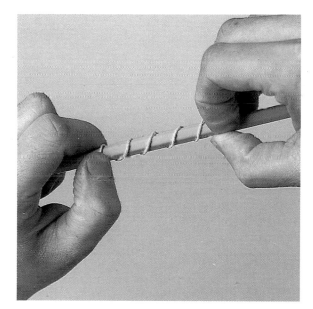

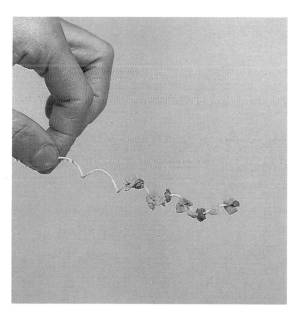

Method 3: Simple Technique for Making Vines on Coiled Wire

You will need:
Several pieces of green cloth
   coated 12-gauge flower wire
Pastry bag fitted with a star or
   plain tip (I used a #13 star tip)
   and filled with royal icing the
   color you want your flowers to
   be
Pastry bag fitted with a #349 (leaf)
   tip and filled with green royal
   icing
Pencil

If you use this method, you won't be able to coat the wire in green royal icing (the icing would crack), so use green cloth-coated wires.

1. Take each wire and coil it around the pencil. Remove the pencil and pull lightly on the ends of the wire to stretch it out a little.

2. With your pastry bag fitted with the plain or star tip, make doughnut-like circles at even intervals on the wire, as explained under Method 1. Using the bag fitted with the #349 (leaf) tip, add sepals and leaves.

Let's Make a
Chocolate-Raspberry Cake!
With Chocolate Whipped Cream and Chocolate Buttercream Roses

Sponge Cake

1 cup sugar
6 large eggs
1 teaspoon vanilla
½ teaspoon salt
1 cup flour, sifted
4 tablespoons melted butter

Place the first 4 ingredients in a double boiler over low heat and whisk them together. Heat the mixture until all the sugar is dissolved and it reaches a temperature of about 120 degrees. Whisk occasionally so none of the egg scrambles along the edge or bottom.

Whip this heated mixture at high speed for about 4 minutes. When the batter falls in thick ribbons, it's ready. Fold in the flour, and then the butter.

Bake in a greased 8" x 2" round pan at 350 degrees for 25 minutes or until golden brown.

Chocolate Whipped Cream Frosting

3 cups heavy cream
¼ cup unsweetened Dutch-process cocoa
3 tablespoons granulated sugar
2 teaspoons vanilla

Whip all ingredients together until the mixture forms peaks. Do not overwhip.

Syrup

¾ cup water
¾ cup sugar
½ cup dark rum (optional)

Boil the water and sugar. Then add the rum, if desired.

Chocolate Ganache

4 ounces chocolate
2 ounces cream
1 tablespoon butter
1 teaspoon vanilla

Chop the chocolate and melt together with the other ingredients in a double boiler over low heat. Don't let the water boil in the bottom half of the double boiler. Stir the mixture as it melts.

Assembling and Decorating

Slice the 8" cake in half (see the cut cakes chapter for slicing instructions). Brush the top and bottom surfaces of both halves with syrup.

Spread a thin layer of raspberry preserves on the top surface of the bottom half, then frost with chocolate whipped cream frosting. Place the top layer on the frosted bottom one, and frost the top and sides of the whole cake with chocolate whipped cream frosting.

Fit a pastry bag with a #2 or #3 (plain) tip, and fill the bag with chocolate ganache. Pipe the ganache onto the top surface of the cake, following the design given below.

Fit a pastry bag with a #18 (star) tip, and fill the bag with chocolate whipped cream frosting. Make a puff border around the lower edge of the cake. For the top, either pipe a series of interlocking "S"'s (to make it look like the cake pictured) or make another puff border.

To make the 4 roses along the border, use a #12 (plain) and #104 (rose) tip and the rest of the chocolate whipped cream frosting. Follow the instructions for making a rose on a "nail" at the beginning of this chapter. When you're through making each rose, cut it off the nail with a scissors, as described in the instructions, and place it on the cake. Put a raspberry dipped in syrup in the center of each rose.

To make the darker rose in the middle of the cake, use chocolate buttercream icing (recipe at the beginning of the buttercream chapter).

"Gather ye
raspberries
while ye may"

Chapter 6

CUT CAKES

You don't have to go out and buy specialty pans to make the cakes in this chapter. All you need are normal round and sheet cake pans and a few empty food cans. I'll show you how to turn the cans into baking cylinders, and show you all the patterns and instructions you need to make 5 fun projects for different occasions.

Arthur darling,
You really have to do
something about Merlin.
Guenevere

Chocolate Castle

King Arthur lived in a chocolate castle, and Guenevere was his bride. Merlin, the resident magician, was always up to no good. Who do you think turned the castle into chocolate in the first place? Arthur made him change it back when he discovered that pieces of the walls and towers were mysteriously disappearing.

All the cut cakes projects in this chapter are surpisingly simple and inexpensive to make. I give you all the patterns and instructions you need to bake, cut, assemble and decorate the cakes.

One of the secrets I use in making the original designs in this chapter is as simple and unassuming as a throw-away can. In fact, that's exactly what the secret is: baking cylinders made out of empty food cans you would normally throw away as trash. It's easy as anything to turn your leftover cans into cylinders you can use to make cylinder cakes for the turrets of a castle cake, or the fuselage of an airplane cake, or dynamite sticks, or anything else your imagination leads you to.

This step-by-step sequence shows you how to make baking cylinders out of empty cans. With a baking cylinder, you can get cylindrical cakes that you could never get from an ordinary pan.

In the instructions, I tell you to grease and flour the inside of the cylinder *and* to roll wax or parchment paper up inside it. Believe me, don't think you'll save yourself time by leaving out one of the steps. The parchment or wax paper allows the cake to drop out of the cylinder easily after baking, and the shortening and flour keep the paper from sticking to the sides of the can.

Keep in mind, when you're assembling your cut pieces of cake, that gaps and seams between them can always be easily filled and hidden with icing.

One last but important point. If you have time, freeze the cylinder cake after you've baked it. This will make it much easier to handle when you get to the frosting and assembling steps.

1. Take empty cans with the tops cut off. Cut out the bottoms of all but 1 of them for each baking cylinder you're making. With the 2 cans I'm holding in the picture, I'll make a 2-can baking cylinder.

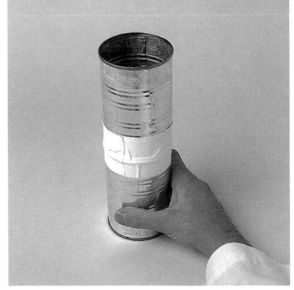

2. Tape the cans together with masking tape.

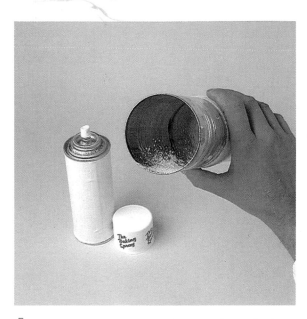

3. Spray vegetable shortening into the cylinder, and then dust with flour.

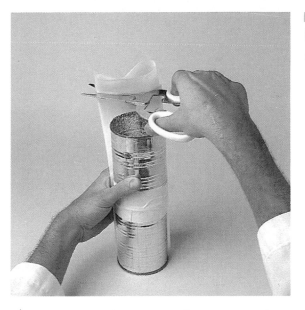

4. Cut a piece of wax or parchment paper about 2" longer than your cylinder.

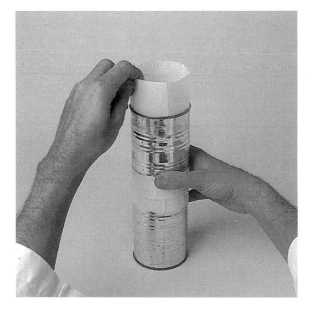

5. Roll up the paper and insert it into the cylinder.

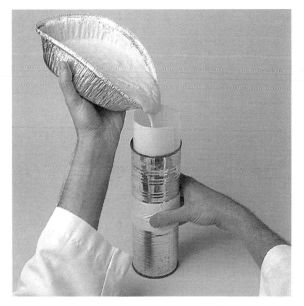

6. Pour cake batter into the cylinder and bake in an upright position. After baking, slice off any cake that has risen above the edges of the cylinder. Turn the cylinder upside down so the cake falls out.

How to Banish Messy Crumbs
That Ruin Smooth Frosting

Crumbs are the bane of the beginning cake decorator. Any loose crumbs on the surface of your cake will get into the icing and keep the cake from being as pretty as you'd like. Of course, the most basic thing to keep in mind when about to frost a cake is that it should always be "swept off" with a pastry brush before frosting. This gets rid of the loosest crumbs. Here are more techniques which you may find helpful in getting the better of crumbs.

The Freezing Technique

After you've baked your cake, let it cool for two hours; place it on a piece of cardboard, and transfer it to the freezer. (If you have a crowded freezer and you're worried about foods coming into contact with the cake, you can wrap it in any convenient material, such as foil or plastic wrap.) When it's frozen, crumbs will stick to the cake instead of getting into the icing.

Freezing is also a great way to store your unfrosted cake. It won't dry out the way it would if kept in the fridge; in fact, I find that they're even moister when they come out of the freezer than when they go in.

Clean Slicing Without Crumbs

When torting a cake or slicing it for filling, a simple way to avoid crumbs is to use the right instrument. You may be tempted to use a serrated knife to slice or torte a cake, but a serrated knife is like a saw. Saws give you sawdust. A serrated knife will give you crumbs. Although it requires a special purchase (since you probably don't have one of these in your kitchen tool drawer yet) you'll save yourself a lot of frustration by buying a slicing knife. If you absolutely don't want to buy one, you can try my dental-floss method. It requires steady hands and a little practice, but the materials are inexpensive and easy to come by.

Crumb-Free Slicing With Dental Floss

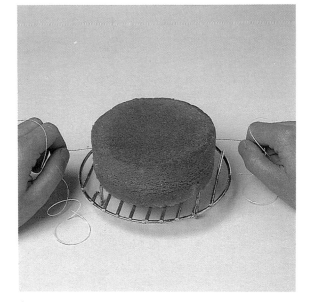

1. Pull unflavored, unwaxed dental floss through the cake with a sawing motion.

2. Before you've cut through the whole cake, cross the 2 ends of the piece of dental floss; then pull it all the way through.

1. Slice through your cake, and slide off the top half.

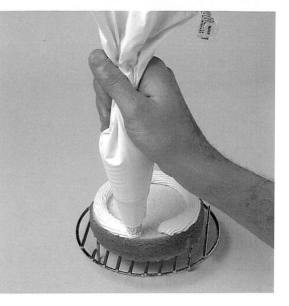

2. Use a pastry bag fitted with any large lip. Fill it with the icing with which you're going to frost your cake. Make a thick line of icing along the edge of the bottom half. This will serve as a dike to keep the filling in.

3. Spoon the filling onto the cake.

4. Replace the top half, and press it down gently.

Chocolate Castle

You will need:

4 batches chocolate buttercream icing (recipe from the buttercream chapter)

9 batches cake mix (recipe of your choice from the appendix)

7 ice cream cones (the pointed sugar cone kind)
 chocolate
 crystalized ginger
 licorice whip
 small chocolate squares
 licorice diamonds

10 12-ounce soda cans, made into 5 2-can baking cylinders (see instructions at the beginning of this chapter)

3 13" x 9" x 2" sheet cake pans

3 12¼"-long dowels
 foil-covered cardboard, about 14" x 18"
 wax or parchment paper
 toothpicks
 brown paper bag
 #18 tip

Baking:

The towers of the castle are baked in 5 2-can baking cylinders. All the other parts of the castle are baked in the 3 13" x 9" x 2" pans.

Cutting, Assembling, Frosting, and Decorating:

1. Place a sheet cake on the foil-covered cardboard base, and follow the first pattern to cut out 3 holes in the cake, using one of your baking cylinders as a cutter.

2. Insert dowels into 3 of the cylinder cakes (the dowels will stick out one end, and give you something to hold on to when you're frosting the towers). Stick the cylinder cakes into the 3 holes you cut in the sheet cake (the end with the dowel sticking out should point up). Frost the sheet cake and the cylinder cakes.

3. Cut the 2 remaining cylinder cakes into unequal halves (about ⅓–⅔). Place the 4 pieces at the corners of the castle, with the shorter ones in front and the taller ones in back. Frost them.

4. Cut the 2 remaining sheet cakes, following the patterns provided. Frost the 4 inner walls and put them in place (look at the floor plan to see where they go).

5. Frost the 6 outer wall pieces and put them in place.

6. Cut a cardboard drawbridge, following the pattern provided. Frost it and slide the end under the front center wall piece.

7. To make the ice cream cone tops of the towers, melt chocolate in the top of a double boiler. Remove from heat, and pour out onto wax or parchment paper. Roll the ice cream cones in the chocolate. Place the cones on a cookie sheet and allow to harden in the fridge.

8. Cut 7 pointed flags out of the brown paper bag, and glue them to toothpicks. Stick each toothpick into the top of a chocolate-covered ice cream cone, and place the cones on top of the towers.

9. With a #18 tip, make a star border around the base of each cone, and along the edges of the drawbridge.

10. "Pave" the castle walls with crystalized ginger. Decorate the walls and towers with chocolate squares and licorice diamonds. Finally, add pieces of licorice whip to the drawbridge.

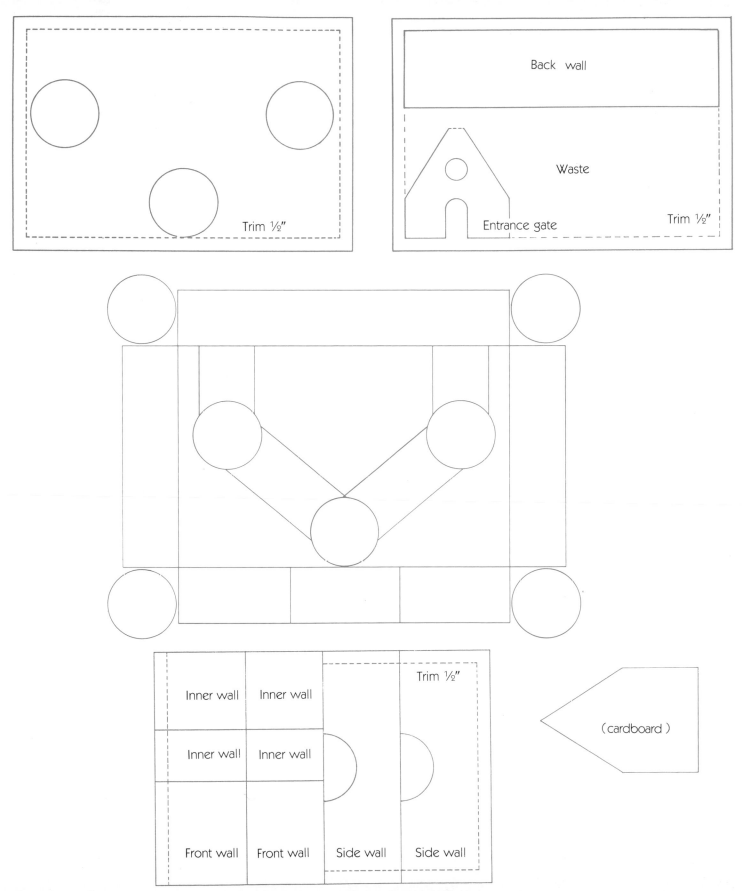

Trim ½"

Back wall

Waste

Entrance gate

Trim ½"

Trim ½"

Inner wall | Inner wall

Inner wall | Inner wall

Front wall | Front wall | Side wall | Side wall

(cardboard)

Paint the Town

What'll it be? Dancing until dawn and cake and champagne for breakfast? Or a sunny housewarming cake to greet a new neighbor? Or a paint can cake for an entirely different occasion, with a message and theme even more clever than these (impossible!)? You're free to choose.

HAPPY HOUSEWARMING

Cher Claude,
When you finish, meet me at the Café Metropole.

Toulouse-Lautrec

You will need:

Double batch buttercream icing (recipe of your choice from the buttercream chapter) for *each* paint can you make (there will be enough left over to frost one paintbrush); make one batch the color you want the can to be, leave most of the second batch white (for the label and handle fasteners), and color 5 tablespoons of it the color you want the writing to be

Double batch cake mix of your choice (see recipes in the appendix) for *each* paint can you make and for each pair of brushes (a 13" x 9" x 2" pan yields 2 brushes)

1 batch filling for each paint can; I recommend my Sweet and Sour Cherry Filling (recipe below)

1 batch double chocolate buttercream (recipe in buttercream chapter) for dark brown brush bristles (optional)

1 #10-size food can (ask for them at a restaurant) for *each* paint can you make

Parchment paper

1 piece of coat hanger wire or wire from the handle of a paint bucket for *each paint can you make*

Circle of foil-covered cardboard for each paint can you make; it should be a little bigger than the paint can

#3, #12, and #18 tips

Sweet and Sour Cherry Filling

1 lb. canned cherry pie filling
1 lb. pitted sour dark cherries, drained
Rind of 1/2 lemon, grated

Baking:

Each paint can is baked in a #10-size food can. The 13" x 9" x 2" pan is big enough to make 2 brushes.

Cutting, Assembling, Frosting, and Decorating:

Paint Can

1. Place a cylinder cake on a foil-covered circular cardboard base. Cut a 2"-deep circle about an inch inside the edge of the cylinder. Scoop out the cake inside that circle with a spoon.
2. Wet a 3" x 4" piece of parchment paper, and stick it onto the side of the cylinder cake.
3. Frost the entire cylinder cake (except inside the hole you cut in the top, and the area where the parchment paper is) with the buttercream icing the color you want your paint can to be.
4. Peel off the piece of parchment paper, and frost that blank spot with white buttercream. Pipe on the words "HAPPY HOUSEWARMING" or

"PAINT THE TOWN" in the color of your choice with the #3 tip.
5. With the #18 tip, make star borders around the white label and around the hole in the top of the can.
6. With the #12 tip, add 2 blobs of white buttercream on opposite sides of the can. Insert the ends of your handle wire throught the blobs and into the cake beneath.
7. Spoon filling into the hole in the top of the paint can.

Paintbrush

Cut out 2 brushes (or 1 brush, if you want only 1) from the 13" x 9" x 2" sheet cake, following the pattern provided. Frost with the leftover buttercream icing you used for the paint can(s). Use the #48 tip for the bristles. If you want dark bristles like the ones on my paintbrush, use double chocolate buttercream.

Pattern for Paintbrush

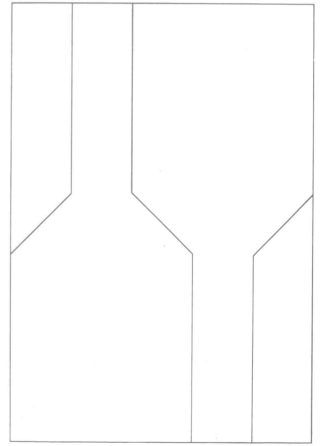

You will need:

- Double batch buttercream icing (recipe of your choice from the buttercream chapter); color all but 5 tablespoons of it red
- Double batch double chocolate buttercream icing (recipe in buttercream chapter)
- 7 batches cake mix of your choice (see recipes in the appendix)—3 batches for the plunger, 2 for the round firecracker cake, and 2 for the dynamite sticks
- 2 chocolate or licorice pastilles
- Red hots
- 13" x 9" x 2" sheet cake pan
- 2 9" round cake pans
- 24 6-ounce tomato paste or juice cans
- —18 of them made into 6 3-can baking cylinders (see instructions at the beginning of this chapter)
- —6 of them made into 3 2-can baking cylinders
- 3 wooden dowels
- —1 about 6¼" long (a little longer than 2 cans laid end-to-end)—2 about 6" long (just as long as 2 cans laid end-to-end)
- 3 pieces of foil-covered cardboard
- —1 rectangular piece about 7" x 9½", for the plunger
- —1 round piece about 9½" in diameter, for the round firecracker cake
- —1 rectangular piece about 4½" x 9", for the dynamite bundle
- white wire
- 7 sparklers or candles
- #3, #4-B, and #18 tips

Baking:

The handle of the plunger is baked in 2 2-can baking cylinders. The base of the plunger is baked in the 13" x 9" x 2" pan. The firecracker in the round firecracker cake is baked in a 2-can baking cylinder. The round base of the cake is baked in the 2 9" cake pans. The 6 dynamite sticks are baked in the 6 3-can baking cylinders.

Cutting, Assembling, Frosting, and Decorating:

Plunger

1. Cut the 13" x 9" x 2" sheet cake in 2 9" x 6½" halves, and place them on the 7" x 9½" foil-covered cardboard base, one on top of the other.
2. Cut a hole about 2" deep in the center of the cake, using one of your baking cylinders as a cutter: push the cylinder straight down into the cake, and then twist it as you pull it back up. The baking cylinder will act like a corkscrew to pull out a piece of cake.
3. Insert the 6¼" dowel into one of the 2-can cylinder cakes. The dowel should stick 1/4" out of

one end of the cake.
4. Drop the cylinder cake into the hole in the plunger base. The end with the dowel sticking out should be pointing up. Frost the base with double chocolate buttercream, and the cylinder with red buttercream icing.
5. Insert a 6" dowel all the way into a 2-can cylinder cake, and frost the cake with red buttercream icing. Lay the cylinder cake horizontally onto the vertical one to form a "T." You'll have to push down gently but firmly so the vertical dowel goes into the horizontal cylinder cake.
6. Add the puff borders. Use a 4-B tip and double chocolate buttercream for the borders around the top and bottom edges of the base. Use a #18 tip for the smaller puff border around the plunger handle. Stud all the borders with red hots. Finally, place 2 licorice or chocolate pastilles on the plunger base, and add positive and negative signs with white buttercream and a #3 tip.

Round Firecracker Cake

1. Place the 2 9" cakes, one on top of the other, on the 9½" foil-covered circle. Cut a 2"-deep hole in the center of the cake with a baking cylinder, as in step 2 of the instructions for making the plunger.
2. Push a 6" dowel all the way into a 2-can cylinder cake, and insert the cake into the hole you made in the round base. Frost the base with double chocolate buttercream, and the firecracker with red buttercream.
3. Make puff borders around the top and bottom edge of the base with double chocolate buttercream and a #4-B tip, and a smaller puff border around the firecracker with double chocolate buttercream and a #18 tip. (I used curved-tail puffs.) Stud the borders with red hots. Finally, insert a sparkler or candle in the firecracker.

Dynamite Bundle

1. Dab or smear some icing onto the 9" x 4½" foil-covered cardboard base. Lay 3 of the 3-can cylinder cakes on the cardboard base. The icing will help keep them from rolling. Frost all visible surfaces of the 3 cylinder cakes with red buttercream.
2. Lay 2 more 3-can cylinder cakes on the first 3, and frost all their visible surfaces with red buttercream.
3. Lay the final 3-can cylinder cake on top, and frost its visible surfaces with red buttercream.
4. Use white buttercream and a #3 tip to "tie" the bundle of dynamite sticks together, and to write the words "HAVE A BLAST." Insert a sparkler or candle into each dynamite stick. Finally, connect the bundle to the plunger with white wire.

Dynamite Cakes

Just imagine . . . You tell everybody to hide, turn off the lights, and light the sparklers just as the birthday boy walks in the room . . . SURPRISE!!! The birthday boy will never be the same again.

Here's where your empty tomato paste cans *really* come in handy. And to think you've been throwing them away all your life.

Dear Lauren,
I think you're
dynamite, kid!
Humphrey

Alligator Cake

Pretty much all you need to make this ugly critter is a single sheet cake, a couple batches of double chocolate buttercream, and a lot of chocolate chips. Turn the page for patterns and instructions. (If you want to make a sandy river bank for your alligator, use turbinado sugar. To find out how to make the water lily, see the candy clay chapter.)

Alligator

You will need:
1 batch double chocolate buttercream (recipe in buttercream chapter)
Double batch cake mix of your choice (see recipes in the appendix)
cake filling
candy corn
chocolate chips
miniature chocolate chips
13" x 9" x 2" sheet cake pan
2 plastic eyes
Foil-covered cardboard, about 26" x 9"
#3 tip

Baking:

The entire alligator is baked in the 13" x 9" x 2" pan.

Cutting, Assembling, Frosting, and Decorating:

1. Follow the pattern to cut out the body, head, tail, and feet of the alligator. Slice and fill the body section (see instructions at the beginning of this chapter). For the filling, I recommend the Sweet and Sour Cherry Filling from the "Paint the Town" project.
2. Place the body, feet, and 2 tail pieces in position on the foil-covered cardboard base. Slice the narrower tail piece (the one for the tip of the tail) to make it slope down and come to a thin point at the tip.
3. Slice the head piece in half to make an upper and a lower jaw. Prop the mouth open with a piece of waste cake. Put the tongue in. Place the head section against the body section.
4. Fill any breaks or dips on the surface of the alligator, then frost the entire alligator. Using the #3 tip, build up eye sockets on either side of the head section, and press the plastic eyes into the sockets. Use the #3 tip to partially cover the eyes with icing "eyelids."
5. Stud the entire alligator with chocolate chips, using miniature chocolate chips on the snout and the end of the tail. Press candy corn into the mouth to make teeth.

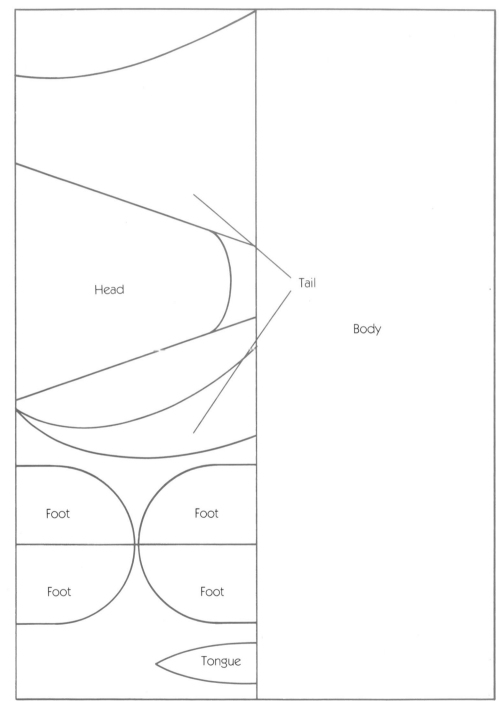

You will need:
  Double batch Butterless Buttercream icing (recipe in
    buttercream chapter); color ⅓ cup blue, ⅓ cup
    red, and ⅓ cup black or brown, and leave the rest
    white
  Double batch cake mix of your choice (see recipes
    in the appendix)
  Piece of sheet gelatin
  chocolate chips
  2 1-lb. coffee cans
  13" x 9" x 2" sheet cake pan
  Foil-covered cardboard, about 2' x 2'
  1 piece of 12-gauge flower wire
  1 toothpick
  Black construction paper
  #3 and #12 tips

Baking:

The fuselage (body) of the airplane is baked in the 2
1-lb. coffee cans. The wings and 3 tail pieces are
baked in the 13" x 9" x 2" pan.

Cutting, Assembling, Frosting, and Decorating:

1. Put a dab of white buttercream on the middle
of the foil-covered cardboard base. Place the 2
cylinder cakes end-to-end on the base, using a
little white buttercream to stick them together. Frost
all but the ends of the fuselage with white
buttercream.
2. Make a snail of white buttercream on either
end of the fuselage, using the #12 tip. Smooth the
surface of each snail with a spatula and water
mister.
3. Follow the pattern to cut the wings and tail
pieces.Place the wings and 2 side tail pieces in
position against the fuselage and frost them with
white buttercream.
4. Frost the top tail piece, and place it in position
on the fuselage. You'll have to press it down gently
but firmly to make it stick.
5. Make red, white, and blue stripes, red stars,
and black or brown lines for the wing and tail
flaps. Use the #3 tip.
6. Cut a propellor out of black construction
paper, using the pattern provided if you wish.
Spear it onto the nose of the plane with a
toothpick. Add a circle of chocolate chips around
the nose of the plane.
7. Cut a 2" x 2" piece of sheet gelatin, bend it, and
stick it into the icing on top of the fuselage
between the wings. Coat the piece of 12-gauge
flower wire with black or brown buttercream, using
the method in the "Flowers on Wire" section of the
"Rows and Rows of Roses" chapter. Insert the
piece of coated wire into the fuselage just behind
the cockpit.

Airplane

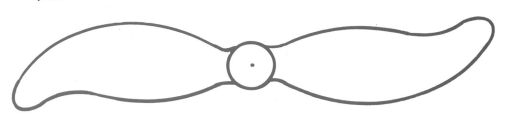

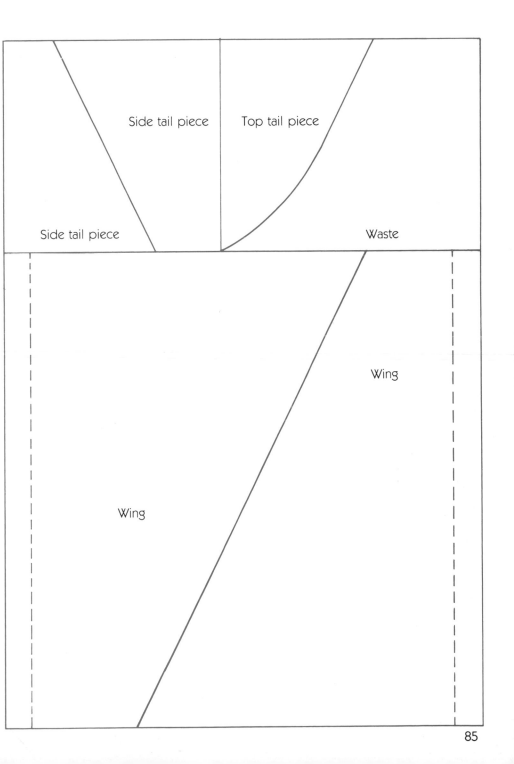

"Bon Voyage" Airplane Cake

Whether it's a top secret Kissinger-esque mission to China, or a week with the grandparents, what better way to begin a trip (or help a friend get off to a happy start) than with this airplane cake? The ones that really fly don't taste half as good.

Dear Dick,

The Beijing caper is on.

Henry

Chapter 7

Cher M. Escoffier,
Don't think your
"marrons" are the
only "glace" in town.
-Mademoiselle Raspberry

ALTERNATIVE ICINGS & TOPPINGS

Up to now, we've concentrated on royal and buttercream icings. This chapter introduces you to many more ways to make a cake smile. A lot of them are not at all fattening.

It is said that, in 1883, a young, talented, and spunky pastry chef named Raspberry crossed the channel and had the effrontery to open a patisserie right across the street from the famous Auguste Escoffier. Chef Escoffier's "marrons glacés" were prized in all the best salons in Paris. The saucy upstart from the "wrong side of the channel" thought she could do Escoffier's glazed chestnuts one better, and sent him one of her stunning glazed fruit-topped cakes along with a note announcing her challenge. The haughty Escoffier merely sent her back another note correcting her French, and saying that he "had no time to look at her cake, and so gave it to the concierge to feed to her children and dogs."

Raspberry, it is said, went on to become just as famous for her "gâteau glacé" as Escoffier was for his "marrons." And justifiably so.

The cake on the previous page is as authentic a reproduction of Raspberry's famed "gâteau" as you're likely to find. (I bet you had no idea what that note meant.) The only thing is, it's not absolutely certain whether she used a fruit preserve or a gelatin glaze on her cake. So you'll find recipes for both on this page.

Glazes

Glazes add shine to the surface of your cake, and seal it the same way that buttercream icing does to keep the cake moist and fresh. But they add little or no sugar and no fat, so they're perfect for dieters or people who find most icings too heavy and sugary.

Fruit Glaze

2 lbs. jam or jelly
¼ cup water
Heat the water in a saucepan (don't let it boil) and slowly add the jelly or jam while you stir. Stir the mixture over low heat until it has become consistently thin with no lumps. Remove from heat.

Gelatin Glaze

1 packet unflavored gelatin
1 cup water
Heat the water in a saucepan (don't boil it) and slowly pour in the gelatin as you stir over low heat until all the lumps are gone. Remove from heat.

Flavored Glazes

Substitute 2 tablespoons lemon juice, cordial, or liqueur for 2 tablespoons water in the fruit glaze recipe; or, substitute ¼ cup juice, cordial, or liqueur for ¼ of the water called for in the gelatin glaze recipe.

All these glazes can be poured right onto your cake; use a spatula to spread the poured glaze evenly. Let it run and drip over the sides or apply it to the sides and spread it even with a spatula. If you're not eating the cake right away, I recommend spreading the glaze over the sides and not just letting it drip naturally, so that the cake is sealed. Always place the cake you're glazing on a cooling rack resting on a jelly-roll pan, so the glaze can run freely down the sides of the cake and drip into the pan below.

Thinly-sliced fruit can also provide a natural, subtly sweet topping for your cake, with gelatin or fruit glaze poured over the slices to make them stay fresh and to seal the cake. If you use fruit glaze, make sure the color of the glaze goes well with the color of the fruit. Apricot-colored glaze looks great on its own, for example, but appears an unappetizing brown color when poured over green kiwi fruit. If you have a wide assortment of fruit on your cake, it's usually best to have either a very pale-colored fruit glaze or a colorless gelatin glaze.

Buttercream Glaze

Buttercream glaze can serve as a complete, light frosting in itself; or, it can be used as a sealant for your cake before you add an outer frosting. This method is great for making your cake easy to frost, since the buttercream glaze seals any crumbs there might be on the cake, so they won't get into the outer frosting that people will see. For more tips on dealing with crumbs, see "How to Banish Messy Crumbs That Ruin Smooth Frosting" in the cut cakes chapter.

To make the buttercream glaze, thin a cup of buttercream frosting with about ¼ cup water. Mix well. Brush the entire cake with the glaze, and let dry 10 to 15 minutes.

Candied Flowers

Let's face it. There's no beating nature when it comes to making beautiful flowers. It's not hard to use nature's own creativity to help you make delicate, edible flower decorations for your cake.

Lots of flowers can be candied. There are two simple rules for knowing which ones may be used. First, and most important, they must be edible. If you don't know whether a flower is edible, any good florist should be able to tell you. Second, thin-petalled flowers are better than thick-petalled ones. Here's a list of a few flowers I like the best:
    violets
    lilacs
    mimosa
    anemones
    small roses
    small lilies
    small variegated carnations.
Edible leaves, such as mint leaves, can also be candied using the same technique used for candying flowers.

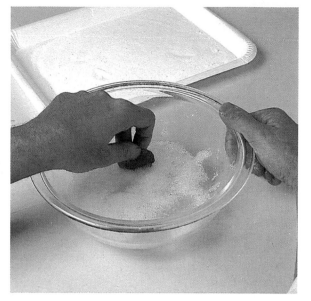

You will need:
3 egg whites
1 cup granulated sugar
Flowers of your choice
Wax or parchment paper

1. Place the sugar and egg whites into separate bowls, and beat the egg whites very lightly with a whisk or fork.

2. Dip a flower in the egg whites. (If you're using large flowers, such as anemones, you might want to pluck the petals carefully from the stem and dip each one separately. Of course, if you do this, you'll have candied flower petals to arrange on your cake, not whole candied flowers.)

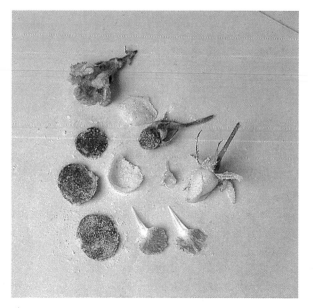

3. Bury the flower in the sugar bowl (the easiest way is to place it in the bowl and pile sugar on top of it so that it's completely covered).

4. Carefully take the flower out of the sugar bowl and place it on the wax or parchment paper. When you've made all the flowers you want, the entire sheet should be placed in a cool area; the flowers will need three days to dry fully.

Whipped Cream and Chocolate Whipped Cream Frosting

These frostings can be spread over an entire cake or used as decorator's icings and piped with a pastry bag to make borders or other decorations on your cake. Here's the recipe:
1 pint heavy cream
1 packet unflavored gelatin
2 teaspoons vanilla sugar
   (If vanilla sugar is unavailable, you can either make your own— I've given you a recipe for it—or use plain granulated sugar.)
For Chocolate Whipped Cream Frosting, you'll need to add 2 teaspoons of unsweetened cocoa powder to the other ingredients in the recipe.

Before mixing, chill a glass or metal bowl and the beaters in the refrigerator for 15 minutes. Place all the ingredients into the bowl and beat at high speed until stiff: if you run a knife through it, the line should be distinct and hold its shape.

How to Make Vanilla Sugar

Take a 1 quart glass jar that is completely clean and dry. Fill about ½" from the top with granulated or superfine granulated sugar. Slice one vanilla bean in half lengthwise and insert into the sugar. Close the jar tight and let sit for several weeks, by which time the bean will have given the whole jar of sugar a vanilla flavor.

14 Minute Eggwhite Frosting

3 cups granulated sugar
1 cup water
4 egg whites
2 tablespoons light corn syrup
2 teaspoons vanilla extract
1 teaspoon salt
Measure all ingredients into a large bowl, and blend together with an electric mixer. Place in top of double boiler with water boiling rapidly in the bottom half. Beat at high speed with a hand-held electric mixer until the mixture forms peaks (about 8-10 minutes).

Cream Fondant

This is a simple-to-make icing that you can pour right onto your cake. It's most often used on the miniature cakes known as "petits fours."
4 cups confectioners sugar
5 tablespoons water
1 teaspoon flavoring extract of your choice
Liquid, paste, or powder food color
Mix all ingredients together at low speed until smooth.

Rolled Fondant

This kind of fondant is called "rolled" because, unlike the pourable cream fondant used on petits fours, you roll it out into a sheet before putting it on your cake. It forms a smooth, durable covering that you can work on with piped icings and other decorations. Here's the recipe:
½ cup water
1 packet unflavored gelatin
¾ cup glucose or corn syrup
scant teaspoon flavoring extract of your choice
confectioners sugar
cornstarch
Warm the water in the top half of a double boiler. Pour the gelatin into the water and stir until dissolved. Still stirring, add the glucose, and the flavoring extract. Place 1 lb. (¼ cup) sugar in a separate bowl. Add the warm liquid mixture to the sugar. With an electric mixer, mix at high speed for about 4 minutes, until it has a stiff consistency, like taffy. If the mixture is stiff but wet and gooey instead of dry to the touch, add ¼ cup more sugar and re-mix at high speed. Test again for a dry feel; it may be necessary to add a final ¼ cup sugar to get the dry, taffy-like consistency.

This has to be stored at least overnight in the refrigerator. To store, dust the inside of a large plastic bag with cornstarch, scoop the fondant out of the bowl and into the bag, tie the bag shut, and place it in the fridge.

You will need:
Batch of fondant (it should have been left at least overnight in the fridge)
Cornstarch
Rolling pin (*preferably* a ridged puff pastry rolling pin; if you don't have one, you can get an inexpensive ridged cloth or cotton rolling pin cover)

1. Sprinkle cornstarch over the counter or board you're working on, and roll out the fondant with the rolling pin.

2. Fold in the edges of the fondant to make a square, and fold the square in half. (This is so the edges of the sheet of rolled-out fondant won't be too rough and jagged.) Roll out the fondant some more until it's wide enough to cover your entire cake (top and sides).

3. Place the fondant sheet over the cake, smoothing lightly against the sides with your hands.

4. Push and smooth together breaks or seams in the fondant with your fingers; a water mister will help fuse pieces together. Cut away excess fondant with a knife.

Chocolate-Peanut Butter Frosting

This frosting is actually a layer of peanut butter covered with a chocolate glaze. The peanut butter makes it more nutritious than most frostings, and the chocolate and peanut butter flavor combination is delicious. Here's the recipe:
1 pint heavy cream
1 cup granulated sugar
8 ounces semi-sweet baking chocolate, broken into small chunks
1 16-ounce jar of smooth peanut butter, put in a warm place ahead of time so it's a little warmer than room temperature and spreads easily

In the top of a double boiler, heat the cream and sugar until the sugar is dissolved, stirring occasionally. Add the chocolate, and stir until it dissolves. Remove the top part of the double boiler and allow it to cool about 10 minutes.

Marzipan

Marzipan is a sweetened almond paste especially popular around Christmas. It can be used as a covering for a cake (it's perfect for covering fruitcake), or sculpted into decorative shapes. Here's the recipe:
1 lb. almond paste
4 cups confectioners sugar
4 egg whites
4 tablespoons rum, or
2 tablespoons rum extract or vanilla

Measure all of the ingredients except half of the sugar into a large bowl and mix at high speed with an electric mixer. Gradually add the rest of the sugar as you mix. When thoroughly mixed, take the mixture out of the bowl, wrap it in plastic wrap, and place it in the fridge for 3 hours to firm up before working with it.

How to Make a Marzipan Covering for a Cake

You will need:
Batch of marzipan
Confectioners sugar
1 cardboard piece, about 12" X 18"
Parchment or wax paper
Thick wooden dowel or rolling pin

1. Place the marzipan on the piece of wax or parchment paper which you have dusted with confectioners sugar.

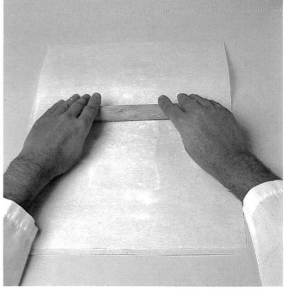

2. Place a second dusted sheet of wax or parchment paper on top of the marzipan. Roll out the marzipan, sprinkling the rolling surface and the rolling pin with more confectioners sugar if the marzipan sticks. Continue rolling until the marzipan sheet is about ¼" thick.

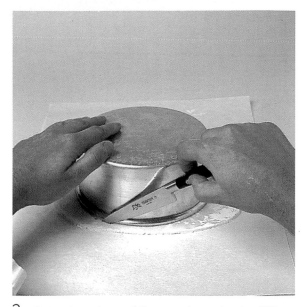

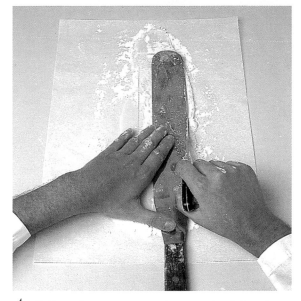

3. Cut out a piece of the marzipan sheet a little bit bigger than the top surface area of your cake. The easiest way is to turn the pan you baked the cake in upside down on the marzipan sheet and cut around it.

4. Ball up the excess marzipan and roll it out again, as in steps 1 and 2. Cut a piece to go around the sides of your cake. The best way is to measure the height of your cake and, using a long spatula or straightedge to get the lines straight, cut a strip as wide as the cake is high.

5. Don't worry if you can't get a strip long enough to go around the whole cake. Just cut it as long as you can, ball up the excess and roll it out again, and cut another strip. When you have enough to go around the whole cake, trim the strips so they don't overlap and lightly press and smooth them together.

6. Finally, press and smooth the top disk to the side strip. Or, if you want to avoid a "pinched" seam, use egg white as a sealing glue where the top and sides touch.

Marzipan Menagerie

You can mold marzipan into any shape you want, just like modelling clay, and then paint it with food color. Egg white brushed on over the food color will keep your sculpture shiny. Here's a farmyard full of animals to inspire you.

Dear Excelente,
You're the cream in
my cup of coffee.

Cupcake

A Cornucopia of Cupcakes

Can you figure out what I used to top all these cupcakes? (Hint: 5 of them have toppings and icings from this chapter.) Look on page 102 for the answers.

Let's Make a
Carrot Cake!
With Cream Cheese Frosting

You'll have to be very watchful if you want to keep this delicious carrot cake safe from the Peter Rabbits around your house.

Dear Peter,
Don't think I don't know
what's going on behind
my back.

Mr. MacGregor

Carrot Cake

2½ cups granulated sugar
1¾ cups oil
3½ cups cake flour, sifted
2 teaspoons single action baking powder
   or 1 teaspoon double action
2 teaspoons baking soda
2 teaspoons ground cinnamon
½ teaspoon salt
4 extra large eggs
3 cups grated carrots
1 cup walnut halves or pieces
¾ cup light raisins
½ cup dark raisins

In the bowl of an electric mixer, combine sugar and oil. Beat until dissolved. Gradually add sifted flour, then add baking powder, baking soda, cinnamon, and salt. Add eggs. Beat until creamy. Transfer the mixture to a large bowl and gradually stir in the grated carrots, walnuts, light raisins, and dark raisins. Grease and flour 2 8" x 2" round pans. Bake at 350 degrees for 1 hour, or until a tester comes out clean.

Cream Cheese Frosting

1¾ cups confectioners sugar
1 cup shortening
1 8-ounce package cream cheese, softened
1 stick unsalted butter, softened
1 teaspoon vanilla

Blend all ingredients with an electric mixer until creamy. Refrigerate for approximately 15 minutes.

Assembling and Decorating

Place 1 8" carrot cake on top of the other, and frost with cream cheese frosting. Press chopped walnuts into the frosted sides of the cake. Make a puff border around the top edge with a #21 (star) tip.

To make the carrots, take the remaining frosting and color half of it orange and half of it green (use paste color). Fit a pastry bag with a #5 (plain round) tip, and fill the bag with the orange frosting. Hold the bag at a 45 degree angle, and squeeze out a line of frosting; lessen pressure on the bag as you approach the end, and then release pressure and pull the bag away. Fit a second bag with a #349 (leaf) tip and fill it with the green frosting. Make leaves on the tops of the carrots.

Answers to Cupcake Quiz

Top row, left to right:
Plastic commercial clown head atop a mound of buttercream piped through a #4-B (star) tip; apricot glaze with buttercream stripes piped through a #18 (star) tip.

Middle row, left to right:
Glazed fresh fruit; lemon cream fondant icing with a candied lemon slice in the center; double chocolate buttercream with a puff border piped through a #18 (star) tip; whipped cream frosting piped in a swirl with a #21 (star) tip and topped with chocolate sprinkles and a marischino cherry; commercial plastic Santa Claus head on red buttercream, with a white buttercream star border piped through a #16 (star) tip; chocolate lace made with a mold (see the chocolate chapter) on top of chocolate buttercream icing bordered with chocolate chips; carrot cupcake frosted with cream cheese icing, bordered with orange cream cheese icing stars piped through a #16 (star) tip and with royal icing carrots.

Bottom row, left to right:
Coffee cup sides frosted with white buttercream after removing the paper, top frosted with double chocolate buttercream, rim made with white buttercream piped through a #12 (plain round) tip, handle made with a frosted chenille wire; buttercream drop flowers made with a #218 tip, #3 (plain round) tip for the center, and a #349 tip for the leaves; yellow roses made on a "nail" with royal icing and using a #101 tip, with the leaves made with a #352 tip after placing the flowers on the cupcake; red royal icing rose made the same way except with a #104 tip; basket frosted with buttercream and topped with mint lentils, French peppermints, and colored crystal sugar, with a chenille wire stem.

Mocha-Almond, Honey-Orange, and Maple Syrup Tofu Icings

Here are 3 high-protein, dairy product-free icings that have the creamy consistency of buttercream. They're all made with tofu, sweetened with unrefined sweeteners, colored with natural plant products, and flavored with a variety of wholesome ingredients. If you have trouble finding any of these ingredients in your usual food market, try a well-stocked health food store.

Like buttercream, tofu icing can be either spread onto your cake with a spatula, or piped with a pastry bag. The Honey-Orange is the stiffest and easiest to pipe; if you want to pipe either of the other ones, you might find it helpful to stiffen it a little by refrigerating it, or increasing the amount of one or more of the powder ingredients called for in the recipe. You could also add some arrowroot, and heat the icing as indicated in the method of the Honey-Orange Tofu Icing. (Arrowroot must always be heated if it is to have a thickening effect.)

The different sweeteners called for in these recipes are more or less interchangeable. Keep in mind, though, that they're not all of equal sweetness, so you'll have to adjust the amount you add if you substitute one sweetener for another. Here are a number of sweeteners you can use if you want to avoid refined sugar, in order of decreasing sweetness: honey, maple syrup, blackstrap molasses, beet and sorghum syrups, barley malt, and rice syrup.

These recipes also call for natural coloring agents, in case you want to avoid the standard, synthesized ones. The Mocha Almond Tofu Icing is colored a dark brown by the carob powder, which also imparts a chocolate-like taste. Turmeric gives the Honey-Orange Tofu Icing a sunny yellow color. The Maple Syrup Tofu Icing has no added coloring agent; its creamy color comes mainly from the maple syrup that gives the icing its sweetness and maple flavor. Beet powder may be used as a red dye, or mixed with turmeric to color an icing orange. You can use unsweetened blueberry preserves to turn your icing a delicate lavender-blue, or the chlorophyll powder from inside a chlorophyll capsule to impart a green color.

One final point: These tofu icings should be made shortly before you use them. Don't store them for longer than 2 days, or the tofu might turn on you.

Mocha-Almond Tofu Icing

1 cup tofu
6 tablespoons beet or sorghum syrup
4 tablespoons smooth almond butter
4 tablespoons carob powder
10 teaspoons powdered instant coffee substitute
2 teaspoons almond extract
1 ½ teaspoons vanilla
Combine all ingredients in a food processor and blend until smooth. Refrigerate when not in use.

Maple Syrup Tofu Icing

1 cup tofu
¼ cup maple syrup
4 tablespoons instant soy milk powder
2 teaspoons vanilla
1 to 2 tablespoons sunflower seed oil or other light oil (optional)
Combine all ingredients in a food processor and blend until smooth. Oil may be added to impart a creamier texture and richer taste.

Honey-Orange Tofu Icing

1 cup tofu
½ cup honey
2 tablespoons sunflower seed oil or other light oil
2 tablespoons arrowroot
2 teaspoons vanilla
10 drops orange oil
½ teaspoon turmeric
Place all ingredients in a food processor and blend until smooth. Pour mixture into top of double boiler and heat while stirring until thick (5 to 8 minutes). As the icing cools, it will become thicker.

Dear Ezra,
"A chocolate rose, is a chocolate rose, is a chocolate rose." Like it?
Gertrude

Chapter 8

Ooooh! CHOCOLATE!

Believe it or not, these red roses are made of chocolate, and they taste every bit as good as they look. In this chapter, you'll find complete instructions for these and many other mouth-watering chocolate confections.

Chocolate Facts:

-All real chocolate is made from the bean of the tree *Theobroma cacao.*

-The word "theobroma" is Greek for "food of the gods." Theobrom*ine* (derived from the genus name of the cocoa tree) is the name of the caffeine-like stimulant found in the cocoa bean.

-The word "chocolate" is derived from the language of the South American Indians who introduced Europeans to the food, in the form of an unsweetened, bitter beverage. "Xocoatl," the Nahuatl Indian word our word "chocolate" comes from, means "bitter water."

-The cocoa bean yields two ingredients used in chocolate: "cocoa butter" (a vegetable fat) and brown "chocolate liquor." *Unsweetened chocolate* has a lot of chocolate liquor and hardly any cocoa butter. *Semisweet and bittersweet chocolate* (which are both *dark chocolate*) have a little more cocoa butter, as well as a little sugar. *Milk chocolate* has less chocolate liquor, more cocoa butter, more sugar, and milk. *White chocolate,* as any true chocolate lover will tell you, is not really chocolate at all, containing cocoa butter, milk, and sugar, but no chocolate liquor.

Chocolate can be a difficult material to work with for someone who's not used to its habits and quirks. Keep in mind that chocolate doesn't take kindly to a hot and humid kitchen. During the muggy New York summer, I'd have a tough time making most of the chocolate confections in this chapter if my kitchen weren't air conditioned. So if you find that the chocolate you're working with is just too droopy and sticky, remember that lowering the room temperature—opening the windows if it's cooler outside than in the kitchen, or turning up the air conditioner—will probably help.

A second important point to keep in mind is that chocolate *hates* water. If any water gets into your chocolate at any point in the melting process, the chocolate will "jam" (congeal) and become unworkable and unusable. Remember that any wet utensils should be thoroughly dried before coming into contact with melting or melted chocolate.

In this chapter, I'll give you instructions for *tempering* chocolate. Tempering is a procedure candymakers use to get their chocolate confections to hold up and look good. It requires precise measurements

with a specialized thermometer, though, so you might want to wait until you become a serious chocolatier before learning the technique. All these chocolate confections can be made with untempered chocolate. Just keep in mind that they'll get gooey if you hold them in your hand too long, and their surface might not be very shiny. When you're ready to learn how the pros do it, try your hand at the tempering technique. It will take a little patience to learn, but with practice you'll find that it's really not too difficult. Don't be concerned that your candies won't look like the ones in the pictures unless you temper your chocolate. All the chocolate confections in this chapter's how-to photographs were made with untempered chocolate.

For all the chocolate confections in this chapter, you may use dark, milk, or white chocolate. White chocolate is a little more difficult to work with than the others, since it takes longer to melt and has a thicker consistency. You might find it helpful to add a little vegetable oil or glycerin to help it along in the melting process and to make it thinner and easier for dipping. You can color white chocolate with paste, powder, or oil-base liquid color. Don't use waterbase liquid color, or your chocolate will jam! (To find out where to get these professional food colors, see the appendix.)

How the Pros Do It: Tempering Chocolate

Tempering chocolate means melting it, removing it from the heat when it reaches a certain temperature, and then allowing it to cool again to a certain temperature.

Tempered chocolate is more stable than untempered chocolate: it can sit out at room temperature without losing its shape or smooth, glossy surface, and you can hold it in your hand without melting it. It's always desirable to temper chocolate you'll be using straight, as opposed to mixed in with other ingredients.

If you want to try your hand at tempering, you'll need a chocolate thermometer to make the precise temperature measurements the procedure requires. The difference between a chocolate thermometer and a regular candy thermometer lies in their temperature range and the fineness of their gradations. A chocolate thermometer is more accurate and easier to read in the range you'll be working in, so it takes any guesswork out of the tempering technique.

1. Chop your chocolate into small chunks so it will melt easily and evenly.

2. Place the chocolate chunks into the top of your double boiler. Heat the water, but *don't* let it boil— boiling water would burn your chocolate and render it unusable. Also, *don't* let any water, even one single drop, fall into the chocolate.

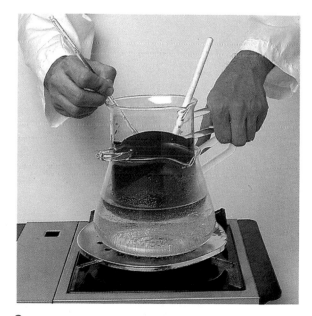

4. When the temperature of the chocolate has dropped to 78 degrees, it is tempered, but too cold to work with. Return the top of the double boiler to the heat, and warm the chocolate back up to 88 degrees. *Don't* let the temperature rise above 92 degrees, or the chocolate will become untempered again! Now your chocolate is tempered and ready to work with. If you use only part of your batch of tempered chocolate, you can put it in a container and store it in or out of the fridge; however, you will have to re-temper it when you melt it again.

3. Stir the chocolate frequently as it melts. When the temperature of the melted chocolate has reached 110 degrees, remove the top of the double boiler and set it aside to cool.

Chocolate-Dipped Fruits

These chocolate delicacies cost a small fortune in New York's posh chocolate shops, but they're surprisingly easy to make. They look and taste great on their own, and really turn your cake into something special.

You will need:
Chocolate
Fruits of your choice (most people like strawberries, pitted cherries with the stems left on, and dried or candied apricots the best); if you wash them, let them dry overnight so there's absolutely no water on them
Double boiler
Wax or parchment paper on a cookie sheet

1. Melt chocolate in the top of your double boiler; don't let the water boil, and don't let any water drip into the chocolate. Remove the top of the double boiler from the heat, and dip each piece of fruit into the melted chocolate so that about ¾ of the fruit is covered.

2. Place each piece of dipped fruit onto the wax or parchment paper- covered cookie sheet. Put in the refrigerator to cool and harden.

Chocolate Leaves

You will need:
Batch of melted chocolate
Real or plastic rose leaves (plastic ones are easier to work with; if you use real rose leaves, paint their backs with vegetable oil so you'll be able to peel them off once the chocolate has hardened)
Artist's or pastry brush or spatula

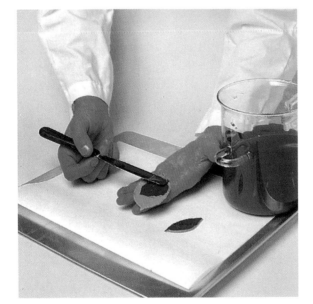

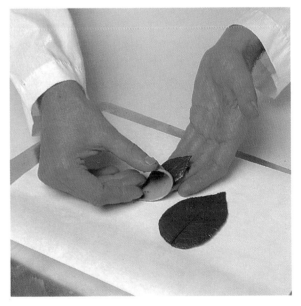

1. Paint the melted chocolate onto the leaves. If you have real rose leaves, paint the back, oiled, side. Paint the chocolate on fairly thick. Place in the freezer for hardening.

2. After the chocolate has hardened, remove from the freezer and carefully peel the leaves from the chocolate.

Using Molds

You will need:
Batch of melted chocolate
Metal or plastic candy molds (if you're using metal molds, let them get cold in the freezer first)
Pastry bag fitted with a tip with a large opening (I used a 2-B)

1. Spoon the melted chocolate into the pastry bag, and pipe it into the molds. Put them in the freezer for the chocolate to cool and harden.

2. When the chocolate pieces have hardened, tap them out of the molds.

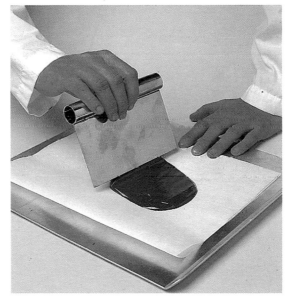

Using Cutters

You will need:
Batch of melted chocolate
Cookie or aspic cutters
Sheet of wax or parchment paper on a cookie sheet
Dough scraper or candy spatula (if you don't have one of these, use a pastry brush or angled spatula to spread the chocolate)

1. Spoon the melted chocolate onto the wax or parchment paper.

2. Use your scraper or spatula to spread the chocolate out into a smooth and even layer.

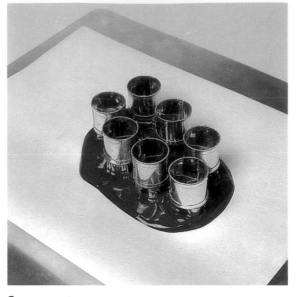

3. Place the cutters on the layer of chocolate so that they cut through the chocolate and touch the paper. Put the entire cookie sheet in the freezer.

4. When the chocolate has hardened, lift the cutters to reveal your chocolate shapes (you may have to tap the cutters lightly to knock out the chocolate). Everything outside the cutters may be saved and reused.

Chocolate Shavings

You will need:
Large piece of room-temperature chocolate
Potato peeler
Wax or parchment paper

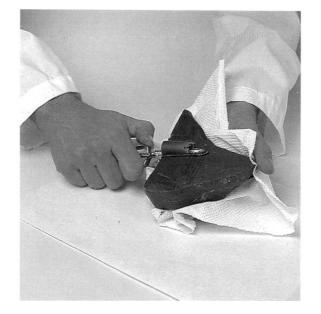

1. Holding the chocolate in one hand and the peeler in the other, shave off curls of chocolate. (If the chocolate is too brittle, warm it up between your hands.) Do it over a sheet of wax or parchment paper.

2. If you want, you can adjust the shape of the shavings with your fingers. Unless you're using these chocolate curls right away, slide the wax or parchment paper onto a cookie sheet and place in the refrigerator. When they've cooled and hardened, you can transfer them to a container and keep them in the fridge as long as you want.

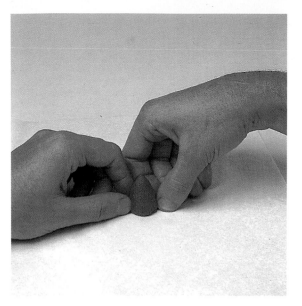

What better present for Valentine's Day, Mother's Day, or your sweetheart's birthday than a cake adorned with a dozen chocolate roses? You can make them any color you choose, including, of course, chocolate-brown.

You will need:
1 lb. semi-sweet chocolate *or,* for white roses, white chocolate *or,* for colored roses, white chocolate and food color (anything except water-base liquid color)
1 cup light corn syrup
Cornstarch
Pastry brush
Wax or parchment paper
Double boiler and heavy saucepan
Thick wooden dowel or small rolling pin

1. Melt the chocolate in the double boiler, stirring frequently. Don't let the water boil, and don't let any water drip into the chocolate. If you're making colored roses, add food color. Heat the corn syrup in a heavy saucepan until warm, pour the warm corn syrup into the chocolate, and stir them together. Remove the chocolate mixture from the heat and stir rapidly until it forms a paste. Refrigerate for one hour, then let sit in a warm place for about 30 minutes to become soft and malleable.

2. Now you can begin to shape your rose. First, pinch off enough of the chocolate mixture to make a conical *base* about an inch wide at the bottom and a little over an inch high.

The cornstarch is for dipping your fingers into whenever you find the chocolate mixture becoming too wet and oily as you work with it. Use the pastry brush to brush off any cornstarch from the surface of the pieces of chocolate mixture you break off and shape.

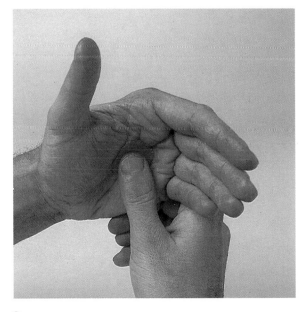

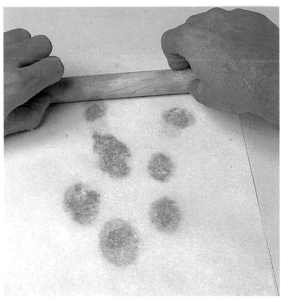

3. Now, you'll start making the petals. For the first, closed petal, make a disk big enough to wrap completely around the base. I find the easiest way is to knead a piece of the chocolate mixture in my palm with my thumb, until I have a flat, thin disk.

4. An easy way to make the disk really thin is to place it between two pieces of wax or parchment paper and roll it out with a thick wooden dowel or small rolling pin. You'll save yourself time if you make about 8 disks (enough for all the petals of the rose), and roll them out together.

111

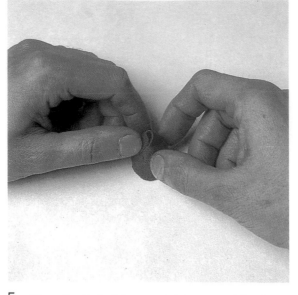

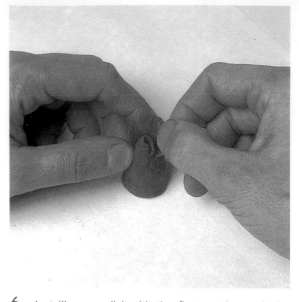

5. Wrap the first disk completely around the base, and press it gently but firmly into the fat part of the base.

6. Just like you did with the first petal, attach the bottom end of the second petal to the base by pressing and smoothing with your fingers. This time, though, curl the top of the petal outwards.

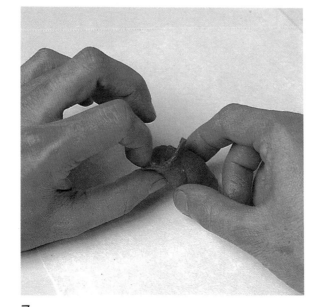

7. When you attach the next petal, make sure it overlaps the first one.

8. Continue to add petals in this way, spiralling them down to the bottom of the base. (If you find that the bottom is too wide and fat, you can pinch off any excess when you're done adding petals.)

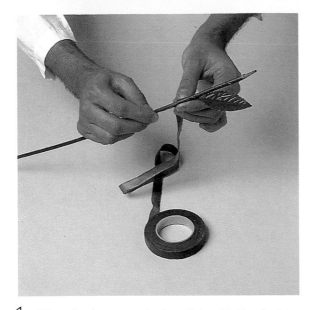

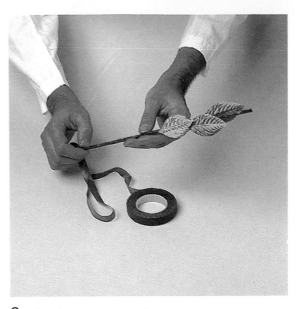

You can use materials available at any florist to turn your rose into a beautiful gift to present on its own to a special person.

1. Wrap the leaves onto the stick with the florist tape. The tape should spiral down the stick. (If you want, you can also wrap dried baby's breath onto the stick.)

2. Continue wrapping the tape all the way down the stick, and cut the tape when you reach the end.

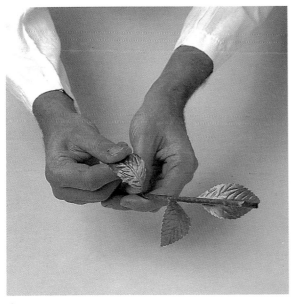

3. Adjust your leaves to make them look natural and pretty.

4. Carefully insert the top end of the stick into the base of the rose.If you want, you can place the finished rose into a rose box.

Let's Make a
Chocolate Book!

Who said that the sensual and intellectual sides of life couldn't be combined? A double chocolate buttercream coating studded with chocolates made in a mold give this weighty tome the look of real tooled leather. The dotted border is made by piping dots of double chocolate buttercream through a #3 (plain round) tip. The "hinges" are made of melted chocolate poured out onto wax or parchment paper and allowed to harden; heat the blade of a small, sharp knife by placing it on a hot stove and cut out a rectangle and a triangle for each hinge. The illusion of pages is created by piping chocolate buttercream through a #48 (basketweave) tip. Or, you can just spread the chocolate buttercream on the sides and make ridges with a fork. Recipes for chocolate and double chocolate buttercream are at the beginning of the buttercream chapter.

Chapter 9
INCREDIBLE CANDY DOUGH

Candy dough is a soft and sweet mixture you can sculpt just like clay. Hence another name you may know it by, "candy clay." It's also called "gumpaste" by some, a name that comes from tragacanth gum, an ingredient used in a centuries-old recipe. The ancient Romans made gumpaste with tragacanth gum (and probably ate too much of it for their own good). My recipe uses gelatin and cornstarch instead of tragacanth gum to make the candy dough "gummy" and elastic. When it dries, the candy dough mixture becomes hard and brittle, just like royal icing. If you take care not to break them, you can keep your candy dough creations for years--unless you give in to temptation and eat them.

Dear Jacqui,
I would have sent a mink but it escaped.
Aristotle

All of these stunning white orchids are made out of candy dough, and are as edible as apple pie. Did I say all? A florist at my elbow tells me one was flown in this very morning from the jungles of Brazil.

Candy Dough

4 cups confectioners sugar
½ cup cornstarch, sifted
½ cup water
½ tablespoon unflavored gelatin
½ teaspoon cream of tartar
confectioners sugar

Mix all the ingredients together with an electric mixer set at low speed. Take the mixture out of the bowl, wrap it in plastic wrap, place it in an airtight container, and set it aside for three hours. Then unwrap it and test its consistency. It should be pliable, like bread dough, and a little sticky but not gooey. If it's wet and gooey, work in some confectioners sugar, a little bit at a time, until the mixture is sticky but not gooey. Candy dough must be stored at all times in an airtight container, since exposure to air will make it dry out and harden. When working with it, break off *only* the amount you need, and return the rest to its container.

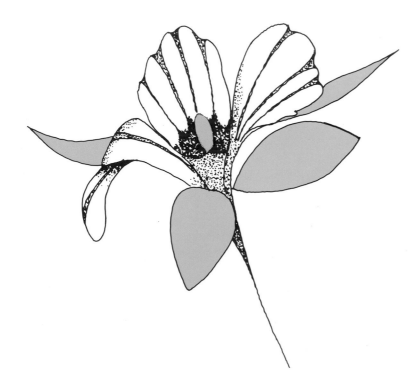

Working with Candy Dough: Rolling out and Coloring

Candy dough must be rolled out before you can cut out the shapes for the flowers I'll show you how to make in this chapter. Before rolling out the candy dough mixture, it is essential to dust your rolling surface and rolling pin with cornstarch. This will keep the candy dough from sticking to any surfaces. Break off just the amount of candy dough you need, and keep the rest in its airtight container. Knead and work it in your hands so its pliability is restored. If it feels too sticky as you knead it, work in some confectioners sugar. The piece of citrus that I mention every time in the list of ingredients is for moistening your hands if they feel too dry from the cornstarch. Lemon, orange, or lime will moisten your hands without making the candy dough gooey and wet.

In the instructions, I'll tell you whenever you need to have *colored* candy dough. The best way to color your candy dough is to break off the amount of mixture you want to color (returning the rest to its airtight container) and knead powder color into it. You can do it without letting any of the straight powder color touch and stain your fingers: put the powder in the center of your candy dough piece and fold the dough over on the powder, so the powder is inside the piece of candy dough. Knead the dough until the powder color is spread evenly through it. The reason I recommend powder color is that it's less messy than paste or liquid. If you do use paste or liquid color, apply a small amount at a time with a toothpick, knead it in, and be sure to wash any color off your hands before working with candy dough mixture you want to stay white.

One final point before starting. In the instructions for making the flowers, I'll often tell you to make *extra* petals or leaves. This is so that, if you accidentally break a piece after you've let it dry and harden, you don't have to make another one and wait another 24 hours for that one piece to dry before assembling the flower.

Patterns for all the flower parts are on pages 130 and 131.

The Lily Pad

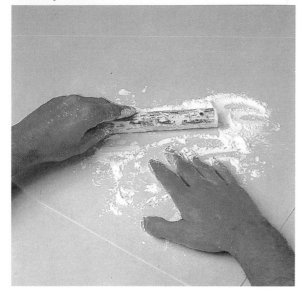

How to Make a Water Lily on a Lily Pad

You will need:
Batch of candy dough
Confectioners sugar
Cornstarch
Green food color, preferably powder
Pastry bag with a little pink royal icing and fitted with a 21 star tip
1 egg white
Thick dowel or rolling pin (preferably small) 2-piece cutter set or a small knife and paper templates made from the patterns provided (see appendix for how to use templates and patterns)
Egg carton
Flower stamens
Piece of citrus

1. Dust your working surface and rolling pin or dowel with cornstarch.

2. Take some of the candy dough mixture and knead green color into it.

3. Roll out the candy dough to a thickness of about 1/16".

4. Using the lily pad cutter or knife and paper template made from the pattern provided, cut out as many lily pads as you want, plus a couple extra in case of accidents. If you use a cutter, make sure it's dusted with cornstarch.

5. Add lines on each lily pad with a knife. Set aside to dry.

1. Roll out some of the white candy dough mixture. With the cutter or knife and template, cut out 2 white flowers for each lily pad you have.

2. If you're using a template, make wiggly lines on one surface of half of the flowers. (A cutter will make the lines for you.)

3. Dip your finger in the egg white, and dab some of it onto the middle of each lily pad. This will act as a glue to hold the flower to the pad.

4. Place a white flower with wiggly lines on each lily pad, and press down.

5. Take the white flowers without wiggly lines and roll them out with your dowel or rolling pin to make them a little thinner.

6. Place the stars in your egg carton. Leave 24 hours. They will dry and harden in a cup shape.

7. When the flowers are dry, take them out of the egg carton and glue them with egg white to the flat flowers on the lily pads.

The Flower Center

1. Squeeze out a dab of pink royal icing in the center of the cup-shaped flower.

2. Insert stamens into the dab of icing. Let dry.

How to Make a Rose

The Flower

You will need:
Batch of candy dough
Confectioners sugar
Cornstarch
2 colors of food color,
   preferably powder: green, and
   the color you want your rose
   to be
1 egg white
Thick dowel or small rolling pin
2-piece cutter set or a small
   knife and paper templates
   made from the patterns
   provided
Piece of citrus

The technique for making a candy dough rose is essentially the same as that for making a chocolate rose. If you need more detailed instructions than those supplied here, refer to the chocolate chapter.

1. Dust your working surface with cornstarch. Knead color into some of the candy dough, and roll it out to a thickness of about ⅛". Cut out 7 or 8 petals. You'll notice in the pictures that I keep the petals under an upside-down bowl. That's so they don't dry out while I'm putting the rose together.

2. Take some of the leftover colored candy dough, and form it into a conical *base* for your rose about 1" high.

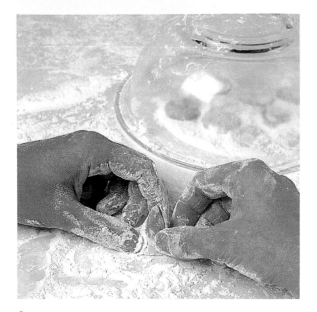

3. Make one of the petals a little thinner with your fingers, and dip it into the egg white (or apply the egg white to the petal with your fingers). Wrap the petal around the base to form the first, closed, petal of the rose.

4. To make the first *open* petal, make another petal a little thinner with your fingers, dip it in egg white, press it into the side of the base, and curl the top of the petal out.

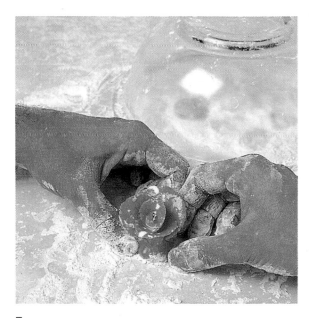

5. Spiral the petals down the base. Make sure to overlap them, rather than placing them side-by-side.

Leaves

For the leaves, work green color into some of the candy dough, and roll it out to a thickness of about 1/16". Cut out a few leaves for each rose you made. (If you're using a knife, make "veins" in the top of each leaf.)

How to Make a White Orchid

You will need:
Batch of candy dough
Green food color, preferably powder
Cutters or a small sharp knife and paper templates for making the leaves and petals of the orchid
12-gauge flower wire
1 egg white
Paper towel roll
Green florist tape
Small child's paint brush
Yellow powder color
1 paper cone for each orchid you make
Piece of citrus

Leaves

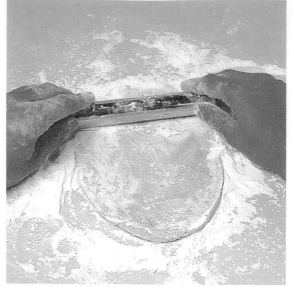

1. Knead green food color into some of your candy dough. Roll out the green candy dough to a thickness of about 1/16".

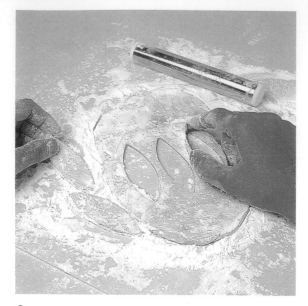

2. With the cutter or knife and paper template, cut out 2 leaves *plus one extra leaf for each flower you want to make.*

3. Dip one end of a 6" piece of wire in the egg white.

4. Press the dipped end of the wire into a leaf, and curl the edges of the leaf around the wire. Repeat for each of your leaves.

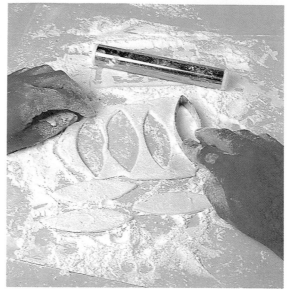

5. Rest each leaf on the paper towel roll, wire side down, so they will dry and harden in a slightly curved shape.

1. Roll out some white candy dough mixture. This time, roll it out about 1/8", not 1/16", thick. Cut out 4 (3 plus 1 extra) petals for each orchid you're making.

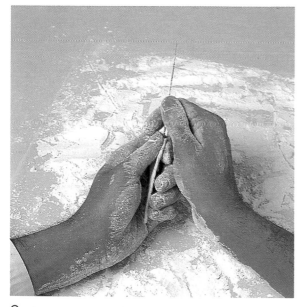

2. Insert a piece of wire into each petal (I used green wire to make it easier to see).

3. Rest the petal on the paper towel roll so it will dry in a curved shape.

Ruffled Side Petals

1. Roll out some white candy dough to a thickness of about ⅛", and cut 2 ruffled side petals out of the white candy dough mixture (plus one extra!) for each flower.

2. Use the end of the paint brush handle to make the edges of the petal look more ruffled.

3. Insert a piece of wire, bend it and the leaf back, and prop it against the roll.

1. Roll out some white candy dough to a thickness of about ⅛", and cut out the center petal.

2. Use the end of the paintbrush to make the edges look more ruffled.

3. Dip your finger in egg white, and apply the egg white to the lower end of the petal.

4. Roll the edges of the petal together, and press lightly to make stay.

5. Insert a piece of wire through the bottom of the petal to make a hole. Take the wire out and set aside.

6. Brush yellow powder color onto the the "throat" or inside of the center petal.

7. Place upside-down on the paper cone to dry.

1. Pinch off a piece of candy dough and roll it between your fingers into a sausage shape. Make one for each orchid; since they're not very breakable, you don't have to make an extra stamen.

2. Take a piece of wire, and make a hook at the end.

3. Insert the hook end of the wire into the stamen, and pull back slightly so the hook will stay.

4. Roll the stamen in egg white, and then roll it in yellow powder color. Set aside to dry.

Assembly

1. Pull the stamen into the center petal.

2. Take the center petal and the 2 ruffled side petals, and twist their wire stems together. Then bind with florist tape.

3. Tape on the smooth petals.

4. Finally, tape on the leaves.

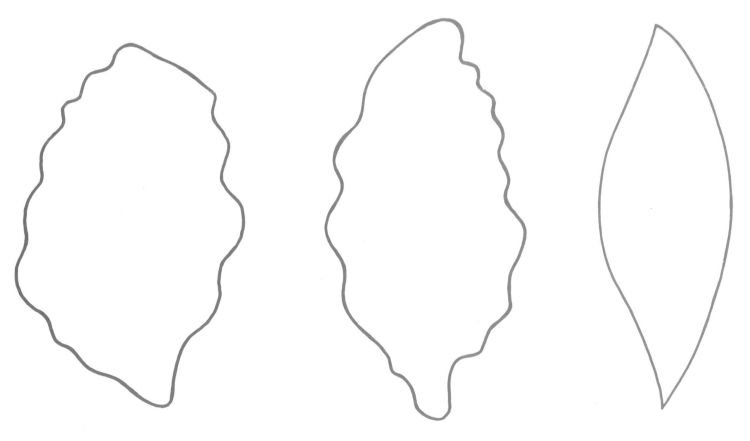

Center Orchid Petal

Ruffled Side Orchid Petal

Orchid Leaf and Smooth Petal

Baby's Dress, Bib, and Umbrella

1 batch of gumpaste is enough for any 1 of these candy dough projects. If you want to make all 3, mix up 2 batches of candy dough. The dress will use 1 batch, and the bib and umbrella will use another batch between them.

Baby's Dress

Make a batch of pink candy dough and roll it out to a thickness of 1/8", following recipe and instructions in this chapter. Cut out 2 bib shapes, following the pattern on page 135 (to make a template from the pattern, follow the instructions in the cookies chapter). Place 1 in an out-of-the-way place to harden. Cut the other right down the middle. Place cotton wool, balled-up foil, or any other available material under the bottom edge and arms of the dress. This will give the candy dough a 3-dimensional, flowing appearance.

When the candy dough has hardened, mix up a batch of white royal icing (recipe in royal icing chapter). Pipe a line of icing through a #2 tip on the underside of the flat candy dough piece along the bottom, sleeve, and neck edges. Press a strip of lace into each of these lines of icing, and set aside to dry. Run a line of icing on the top surface of the other candy dough piece along the bottom, sleeve, and neck edges. Press lace into the icing. Pipe a line of dots to cover the seam between the lace and the candy dough. Pipe swags, squiggles, and dots of icing as suggested in the pattern. Press 2 pieces of ribbon into a dab of royal icing at the neck of the dress. Make 2 royal icing drop flowers on the spot where the ribbons are attached to the dress, and a few more lower down on the front of the dress. Use a #218 tip for the drop flowers, a #2 or #3 tip for the drop flower centers, and a #349 tip for the leaves. Finally, place the top, wavy-edged part of the dress onto the bottom, flat part. Use a little royal icing to stick them together.

Baby's Bib

Mix a batch of white candy dough and roll it out to a thickness of 1/8". Cut out a bib shape, following the pattern on page 136. Prop a few spots along the edges of the bib with cotton wool or foil, to give it a wavy look. After the candy dough has dried, use blue royal icing piped through a #3 tip to make a border, and to make blue dots on the surface of the bib. Add drop flowers, using a #218, a #2 or #3, and a #349 tip, as for the baby dress drop flowers. Finally, tie a blue ribbon through the holes at the top of the bib.

Baby's Umbrella

Mix a batch of yellow candy dough, and roll it out to a thickness of 1/8". Cut out a circle about 7" in diameter, and scallop the edges. Cover a grapefruit or similar-sized round object with foil, and wrap the candy dough circle over it. If you create any unevenness in the candy dough, use a water mister to help you smooth it out again. When the candy dough is hard, use the method described in the instructions for making the baby's dress to attach lace to the edges of the unbrella. Pipe fine squiggly lines of yellow royal icing along the edges and frame, or "ribs," of the umbrella. Add a drop flower or 9. Make the handle out of a pipe cleaner with satin ribbon wound around it. Attach it by pressing it into a dab of icing in the middle of the underside of the umbrella. Tie on a yellow ribbon.

Rose Leaf

Water Lily Pad

Water Lily Flower

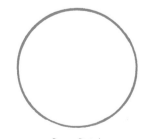

Rose Petal

Instructions for making these exquisite candy dough creations are on page 131. You'll find patterns on pages 134 and 135. To make the cake pictured, mix up a double batch of cake batter (recipe of your choice from the appendix), and bake 2 12" round cakes. Frost with white buttercream icing, and use a #18 (star) tip to pipe borders of curved-tail puffs around the top and bottom edges of the cake. Add drop flowers with a #223 tip, a #3 tip for the drop flower center, and a #349 tip for the leaves.

Let's Make a
Baby Shower Cake!

With Candy Dough Baby Dress, Bib, and Umbrella

IT'S A BOY

Dear Jocasta,
Can't wait to meet you.
Your devoted son-to-be,
O.R.

Pattern for Candy Dough Bib

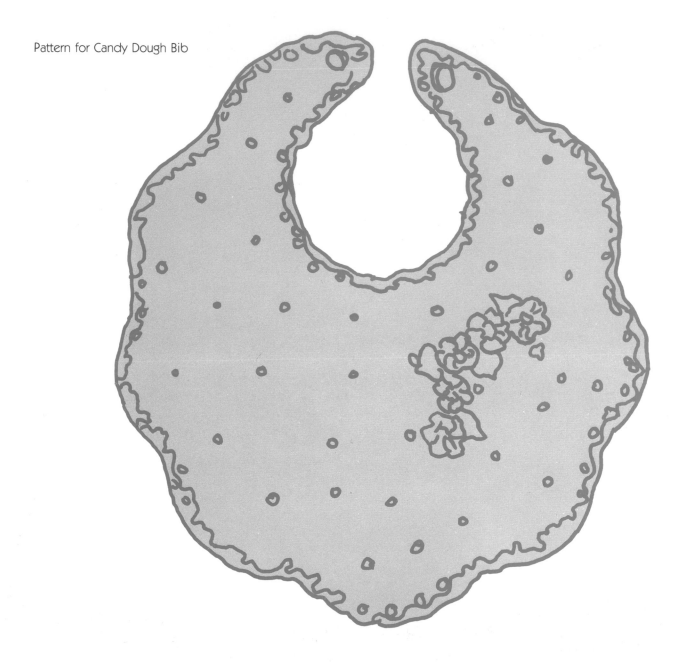

Pattern for Candy Dough Dress

Chapter 10
THE MAIN EVENT

Dear Cinderella,

Please hurry!

Prince Charming

Everybody knows that making a wedding cake is an elaborate and difficult production best left to an experienced expert. Right?

Wrong! This chapter is an inspirational gallery of wedding and anniversary cakes ranging from the challenging to the downright simple.

This Cinderella wedding cake adorned with yellow orchids, for example, requires only the skills that you learned in the very first chapter of this book. It's a perfect example of the way that exquisite flowers can turn an otherwise ordinary cake into a masterpiece.

Simply place a 12" cake on a 13" separator plate (available in cake decorating supply stores) and frost it with white buttercream. Place a 10" cake on top of that, frost, and place an 8" cake on the very top and frost it. Make borders of curved-tail puffs with a #21 (star) tip, and stud with silver dragees. Finally, add the flowers.

That's all there is to it!

The horses and carriage are made with royal icing piped onto tulle fabric attached to a wire frame. Turn the page for instructions.

How to Use Royal Icing on a Wire and Tulle Framework

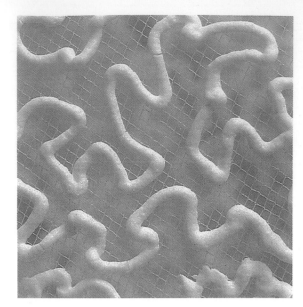

Cinderella's horses and carriage, and the seashell on the opposite page, are made by gluing tulle fabric to a wire frame, and piping squiggles of royal icing onto the fabric. You can buy wire frames in craft stores, or make them yourself with coat hanger wire and a pair of pliers. Tulle fabric is available in sewing and fabric stores.

The close-up picture at right shows the design of the icing squiggles. Pipe the royal icing through a #2 or #3 (plain round) tip. Use a #16 tip to make star borders along the wire frame.

How to Make Stringwork

This picture shows the technique for making "string-work," which I used on the seashell-topped wedding cake on the opposite page, and on my miniature anniversary cake on page 140. Touch the tip to a puff or star on the side of the cake as you begin to squeeze out icing, and continue to apply even pressure on the bag and squeeze out icing as you move the tip towards the next point from which the string will hang.

Until you reach that point and attach the end of the string to the cake by touching the tip to it, the string of icing is suspended between the starting point and your tip. You can make a simple series of single strings around your cake, or do overlapping stringwork, or suspend a small string loop from each point where the stringwork is attached to the cake.

This wedding cake is decorated entirely with a #21 (star) tip and a #3 (plain round) tip. The seashell on top holds a bouquet of orchids and baby's breath.

Place a 10" cake on a 11" separator plate, and frost with white buttercream, then place an 8" cake on top of that, and frost it. The puff borders, and the puffs and stars to which the stringwork is attached, are all made with a #21 (star) tip. The stringwork is piped through a #3 (plain round) tip.

Something old,
Something new,
Something borrowed,
thing blue.

Dear Mr. + Mrs. Swift,
Congratulations on your
25th anniversary.
Gulliver

This lilliputian anniversary cake is a perfect size for 1 happy couple to share. The bottom layer is just 3" across, the middle one 2", and the top later is a mere 1" from edge to edge. You ask how I found cake pans so small? Well, I didn't need to. 1", 2", and 3" just happen to be standard biscuit cutter sizes. I half-filled a 13" × 9" × 2" sheet cake pan with cake batter, and cut out the 3 tiny cakes after baking.

The puffs are all made with a #16 (star) tip, the stringwork with a #2 (plain round) tip, and the drop flowers with a #218, #349, and #2 tip for the petals, leaves, and center. The mound of drop flowers on top of the cake is sprouting a tiny spray of flowers on wire.

How to Assemble a Tiered Wedding Cake With Separator Plates and Columns

This sequence shows you how to use separator plates and columns to make the 3 tiered wedding cakes pictured on the pages that follow.

In the how-to shots, I use styrofoam cylinders to represent round cakes. The pegs, plates, and columns I use in this sequence are all available in standard kits from any cake decorating supply store.

1. First, place your bottom layer on a separator plate that's 1" bigger than the cake, and frost the cake. Attach pegs to a second separator plate that's 1" smaller than the diameter of the cake.

2. Sink the pegs into the cake, and push down until the separator plate is resting on the surface of the cake.

3. Put the columns in position.

4. Put the next layer on a separator plate that's 1" larger than the cake that will rest on it, frost it, and place it in position on top of the columns.

The carnation wedding cake with kissing figurines on the previous page is made from an 8" cake resting on columns atop a 12" cake. The puff and star borders are made with a #21 (star) tip, as are the ridges wavy lines on the sides of the cake. The thick dots and the plain wavy lines on the sides of the cake are made with a #9 (large plain round) tip. Both tiers are adorned with an assortment of ribbons and flowers, including carnations, rosebuds, and baby's breath. A spray of flowers on wire cascades over the top. The kissing figurines are available in bridal shops, cake decorating supply stores, and gift shops.

Some of the flowers on this cake are real, but 7 pink rosebuds are made of candy dough. Can you find them? To make candy dough rosebuds, follow instructions in the candy dough chapter for making the base and first, closed, petal of the rose, instead of going on from there to add the open petals, attach 2 more closed petals.

The cake on the bottom tier is 10", the next one is 8", and the top is 6". They're all frosted with white buttercream textured with paper towels (see how-to instructions in the buttercream chapter). The puff borders are made with a #21 (star) tip.

The bells and figurines are available in cake decorating supply stores, gift shops, and bridal shops. To attach the bells, just loop a piece of wire through the top and insert the ends of the wire into the cake.

Querido Mama,
Though I miss you, Papa,
and our beautiful Aragon,
your lovely flowers will
always be a sweet memory
for Henry and me.
Catherine

Dear Mother,
It was beautiful!
And Adam says his
dad will get over it.
Love,
Eve

Like the very first cake in this chapter, this cake shows the ability of flowers to transform the appearance of a wedding cake. The basic cake is as simple as can be, but the orchids and baby's breath turn it into a dreamy, romantic wonder. Did you notice something else? If you flip back a page, you might notice that this is the same cake pictured there—and yet, its look is completely different. By substituting a simple arrangement of ribbon, baby's breath, and purple orchids for a profusion of flowers, bells, and kissing figurines, I've turned a playfully romantic wedding cake into a subtle, dreamy one.

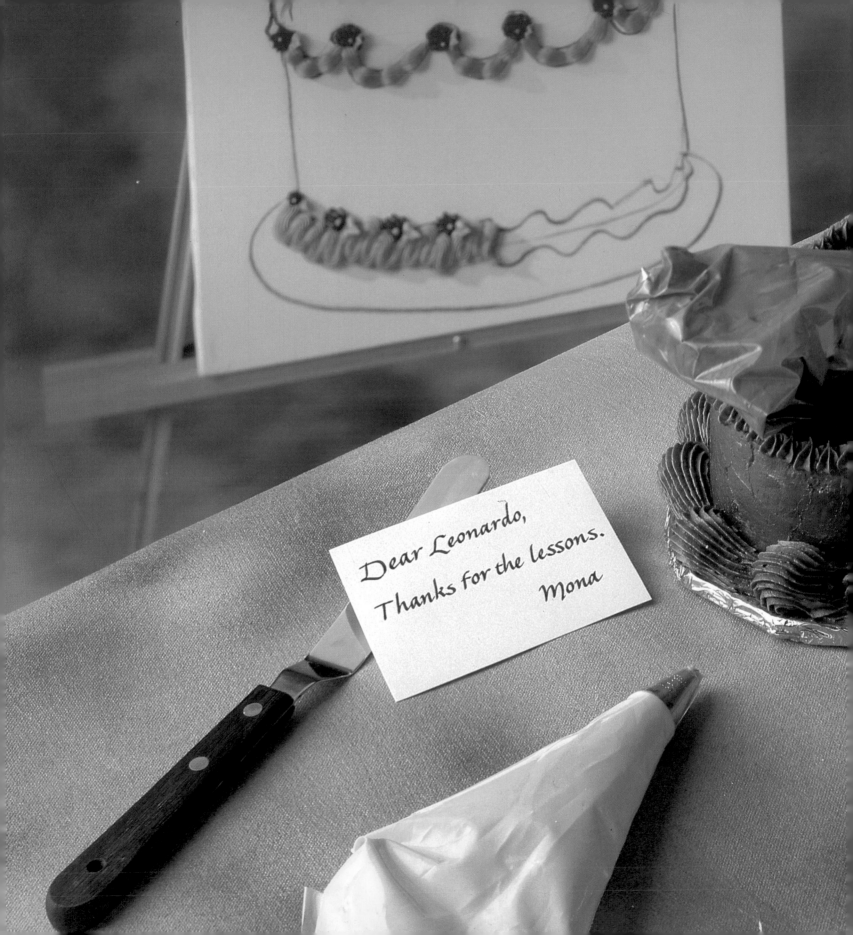

Dear Leonardo,
Thanks for the lessons.
Mona

You could say that the cake decorator is an artist who paints with spatulas and pastry bags instead of brushes. Well, come to think of it, cake decorators do use brushes—pastry brushes, artist's brushes, and small children's paint brushes. Not to mention tip brushes. In fact, cake decorators use an awful lot of equipment.

This palette cake, by the way, is cut out of a 12" X 9" sheet cake, and decorated with a minimum of icing. The sides are frosted with chocolate buttercream (the recipe's in the buttercream chapter). The star border along the top is made with chocolate buttercream piped through a #21 tip. The puff border around the bottom edge is piped through a #3-B (large star) tip. A few dabs of buttercream in a variety of colors complete the cake.

Tools of the Trade

Those beautiful cakes you always wish you could make yourself aren't created with fancy tricks or gadgets. Even the most elaborate multi-tiered wedding cakes are put together with a few basic tools and ingredients used the right way. The premise of this book is that there is always a "right way" that is also an easy way. In this section, I'll introduce you to some of the materials you'll be using, and give you some general information about using them the right way.

Almost all of these materials are available at any cake decorating supply store. (I say "almost" because not many cake decorators have caught on to the fact that a water mister is a wonderful tool for helping frost a cake.) If you have any difficulty finding them, try the mail-order supply houses listed at the end of the book.

Spatulas

As you probably know already, the word "spatula" refers to two quite different sorts of animal lurking within your kitchen tool drawer. A spatula can be either a rubber (or plastic) paddle-like curiosity, or a long and nobly glistening metal instrument. Unless otherwise indicated, whenever I use the word in my instructions, I mean the long metal kind.

Metal spatulas can be used for mixing ingredients, but have a more important role in spreading and smoothing icing on a cake. Correct use of the spatula, and choice of the right spatula, are essential for creating a smooth decorating surface on your cake.

Like a painter's brush, metal spatulas come in a variety of shapes and sizes, each one best suited to a particular task. Small straight spatulas can be used to spread icing over a small area, such as the tops of cupcakes; they can also be used to mix a coloring agent into a small amount of icing. Large straight spatulas are used for spreading icing on cakes. The larger the spatula, the greater the surface area that can be covered in one sweep. Angled spatulas are helpful for working on hard-to-reach surfaces, and for fixing mistakes you discover after much or all of your cake has been frosted and decorated. The angle allows you to reach just the part you want to fix, without touching or smudging areas you want to stay as-is. When you scrape off "HApy BirhdaY jOHn" with an angled spatula, your buttercream puff border will remain unharmed.

Tips when buying spatulas: Look for a stainless steel blade attached to the handle by rivets (not glue) and with enough flexibility to bend somewhat with the curve of your cake.

Water Mister

I find a mister to be an indispensable tool for getting a smooth, even surface on my frosted cake with a minimum of fuss and effort. As you spread your buttercream icing with a spatula use the mister to spray the icing with water. This keeps the icing from sticking to your spatula—usually a frustrating problem, especially for beginners. The reason this works so well is that the water is repelled by the shortening in the buttercream icing, so that there's actually a film of water between the spatula and the icing. Don't worry about spraying on too much or too frequently: since the water is repelled, it won't thin the icing or make it runny, and it'll just evaporate when you're through frosting. See the buttercream chapter for step-by-step how-to's.

Slicing Knife

A slicing knife is used for slicing layer or filled cakes. Chances are you don't have one in your kitchen yet, and you'll be tempted to use a serrated knife instead. A serrated knife, though, makes lots of crumbs, and crumbs are the last thing you want on your cake when you're trying to frost it. You'll save yourself a lot of frustration if you use a real slicing knife.

Pastry Bags

These are the bags you pipe your icing out of to make all those fancy rosettes and flowers and puff borders on your cake. There are several kinds of pastry bag available to you, each with its own advantages and disadvantages. They fall into two basic categories, disposable and non-disposable.

The main advantage of disposable bags is their convenience: after you use them, you simply throw them away. A major disadvantage, though, is that they have a tendency to break if you try to use a *coupler* in them (more about couplers later in this section); as you'll find out, this seriously restricts their usefulness and versatility. In fact, they tend to break under any significant pressure, so they should really only be used for a small amount of icing.

Parchment bags are disposable bags made from parchment triangles you roll up yourself.

1. This is the flat parchment triangle, with the corners marked A, B, and C.

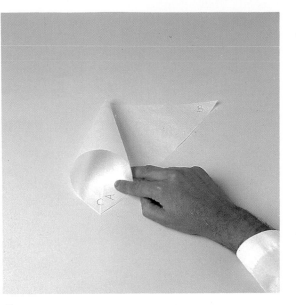

2. Curl corner A around so that it meets corner B.

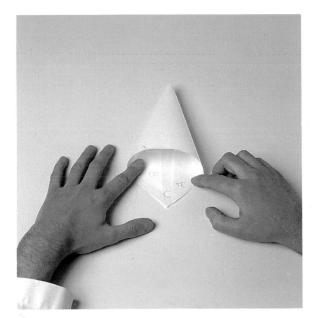

3. Curl the corner B around so that it meets the other two.

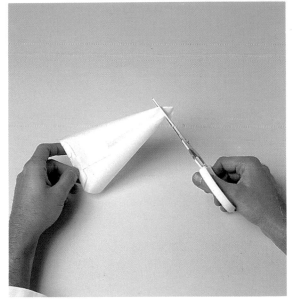

4. Fold down the pointed part where the 3 corners meet, and tape it down. Cut about ¾" off the end to accomodate your decorating tip.

Plastic disposable bags come ready-rolled; like the parchment bag, they must be trimmed to accomodate a decorating tip.

There are 4 kinds of non-disposable bags: canvas, plastic-coated canvas, polyethylene, and French nylon.

I'd stay away from canvas bags, as the material is so porous that icing will seep through and get onto your hands.

Plastic-coated canvas bags are better, since the plastic prevents any seepage. If you use couplers in them, though, you'll have to trim the end of the bag and sew on a hem so the fabric won't unravel.

Polyethylene (heavy plastic) bags don't have to be trimmed to accomodate couplers, and they're reinforced at the tip so they won't break or fray. However, I don't like to use them because of their slick plastic feel.

French nylon bags are my favorite (they're also preferred by most professionals). They accomodate couplers without any adjustment, won't leak, can be cleaned in the dishwasher or washing machine, and are soft to the touch.

You can use this information to equip yourself with pastry bags you think best fit your needs. I recommend getting a few nylon bags and a good supply of plastic disposable bags or parchment triangles. Nylon bags cost a little more than other pastry bags, but they work the best and last the longest. The disposable bags will be good for piping gel, touch-ups, and small fancy additions requiring minimal amounts of icing, as well as for coloring techniques that would stain your non-disposable bag.

If you need to see how to fill a pastry bag, you'll find a how-to sequence in the buttercream chapter.

Decorator's Turntable

A turntable allows you to work on different parts of your cake from different angles without risk of smudging or damaging the cake while moving it. It's especially helpful when making a continuous border around the edge of your cake. I recommend a metal turntable, as plastic turntables tend to break under the weight of a large cake. To be able to work on the sides of the cake at eye level, use a turntable that raises the cake at least six inches from the table top.

Pastry Brush

A pastry brush looks just like a housepainting brush. I use mine for just about everything *but* painting walls. It's perfect for brushing the crumbs off a cake you're about to frost, for spreading melted chocolate when you make chocolate decorations, for dusting extra cornstarch off chocolate roses, and on and on. It's one of the most useful and versatile cake decorating tools I have in my kitchen.

Couplers

Couplers are the cake decorator's most helpful invention since the pastry bag. They allow you to change your decorating tip without having to change the whole bag. That way, you can go from, say, making stars with pink buttercream to making pink buttercream drop flowers without having to empty all the pink buttercream out of the bag to change tips, or transfer all the icing into a second bag with a drop flower tip. All you do is unscrew the coupler ring to release your star tip, put on a drop flower tip, and screw the ring on again to hold the tip in place. To see how to use a coupler, see the step-by-step how-to's in the buttercream chapter.

Couplers come in 2 basic sizes, small and large, to accomodate small or large tips. Most of the tips you'll be using will fall into the smaller group, so the smaller coupler is the more important one for you to have.

What do you do when you have to change from a small to a large tip, or vice-versa? Well, with the basic 2-part coupler unit, you have to change the coupler. This means using a second bag or removing your icing, changing the coupler, and putting the icing back in again. That's exactly what the coupler was designed to avoid in the first place!

It was with this problem in mind that some bright individual came up with the idea of the *interchangeable coupler* (also known as the 5-part coupler). The interchangeable coupler allows you to go from one tip size to another without much fuss at all. Here's how it works:

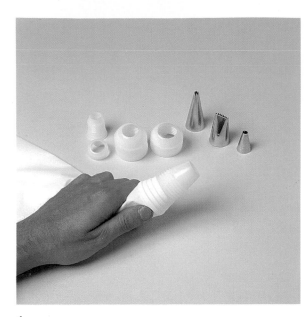

1. The interchangeable coupler consists of a large base, a small base, and large, medium, and small rings. First, put the large base in the bag.

2. The largest ring is used to attach the largest tip.

3. The medium ring is used to attach the slightly smaller tip.

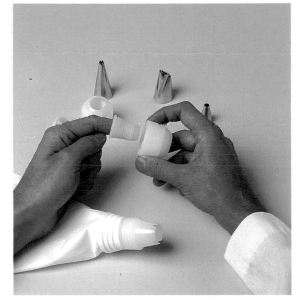

4. To attach the small tip, put the small base in the biggest ring.

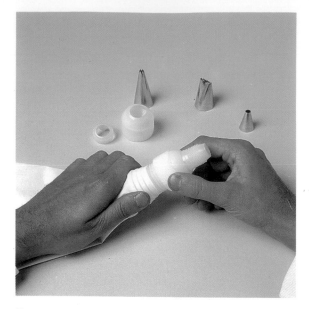

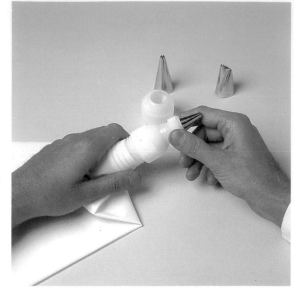

5. Screw the ring onto the large base in the bag.

6. Attach the small tip to the small base with the small ring.

Tips (also known as tubes)

All the agonizing over kinds and sizes of pastry bags and couplers would be for naught without this final, crowning element: the tip.

Tips come in so many shapes and sizes that a full array of them would be perplexing to any beginning cake decorator. Once you've seen how they fall into a few basic groups according to the shape of their opening, though, you'll be able to make sense of the mass of tips at your disposal.

The tip chart shows the categories most tips fall into, and gives you examples of the kinds of shapes and designs you can make with them. The chart, of course, is merely meant to give you a rough idea of the basic kinds of tips there are and what they can be used for, not to show you exactly how to make the designs pictured. You'll find detailed instructions throughout the book.

When buying tips, I recommend getting the imported, not domestic, kind. Imported tips are rust-proof, while domestic tips must be dried carefully after washing to prevent them from rusting.

Tip Brush, Tip Stick, and Tip Cap

The tip brush, stick, and cap are aids to keeping your icing coming through the tip the way it should. When you have a pastry bag full of icing and you have to set it aside, place a cap over the tip. The cap prevents air from getting to your icing and drying it out. A tip stick is for cleaning bits of dried icing from the tip opening. The tip brush is for cleaning out the tip when you're washing it.

Tips Chart

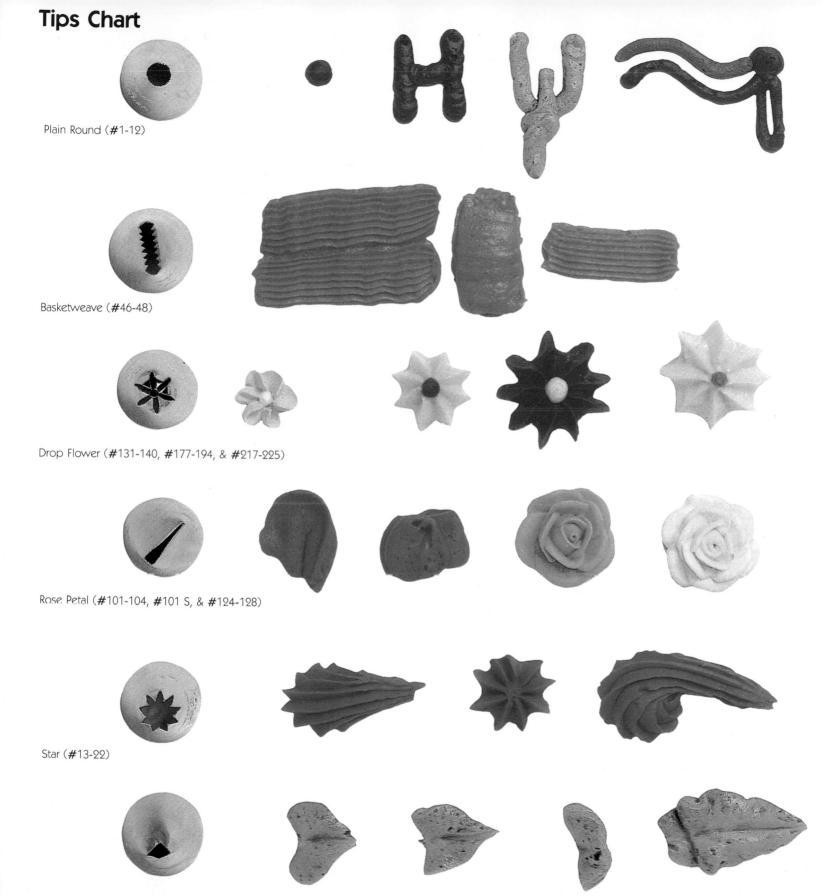

Plain Round (#1-12)

Basketweave (#46-48)

Drop Flower (#131-140, #177-194, & #217-225)

Rose Petal (#101-104, #101 S, & #124-128)

Star (#13-22)

Leaf (#349, #350, & #352)

155

Practice Sheet

Lay a piece of wax or parchment paper directly over these designs and practice your technique. They're photographed same-size, so you can reproduce them precisely if you use the tip indicated.

Puffs & Stars (#21 tip); Stringwork (#3 tip)

Curved-Tail Puff Border (#21 tip)

Puff Border (#18 tip)

Interlocking Stars (#18 tip)

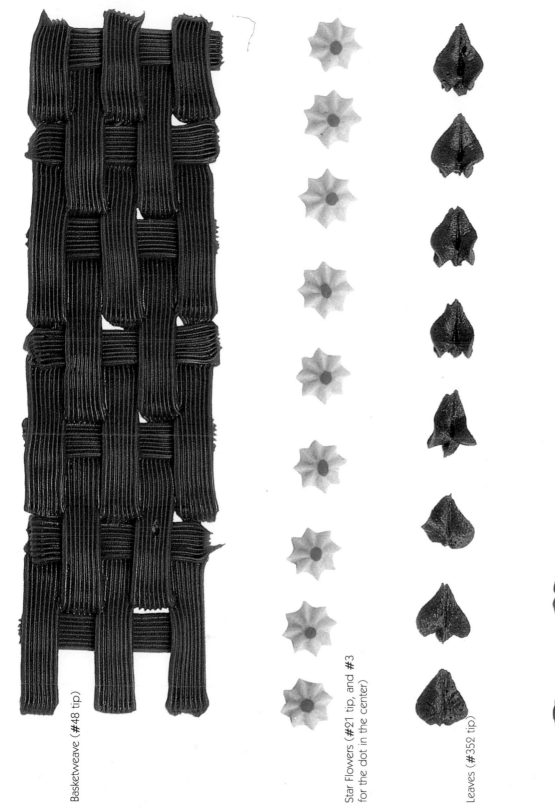

Basketweave (#48 tip)

Star Flowers (#21 tip, and #3 for the dot in the center)

Leaves (#352 tip)

Puff Border with Dragees (#21 tip)

Fleurs-de-lis (#18 tip)

Colors and Coloring Techniques

There are three kinds of coloring media the cake decorator can use to color icing: liquid, paste, and powder. You must keep in mind that none of these is available at supermarkets, and they must all be purchased at a bakery or cake decorating supply house.

Coloring Buttercream:

Any of the three kinds of coloring media may be used to color buttercream icing, but each has advantages and disadvantages you should know about. The greatest advantage of paste and powder is that they won't change the consistency of your icing. Powder has the added advantage of being dry, so it won't stain your hands. Neither powder nor paste is as concentrated as professional liquid color, though, so they are best used for light colors and pastels. You *could* simply add a large amount of paste or powder to achieve a deep color, but you would then risk having the taste of the coloring agent (many paste colors are noticeably bitter) come through in your icing. Liquid colors (*not* the watered-down liquid food colors available in supermarkets) are the most concentrated of the three kinds, so you need less. The only drawback is that addition of liquid color increases the liquid content of your icing. This is usually no problem when using a small amount of liquid color, but if you want to achieve a deep shade, you can do one of two things. The water content called for in your icing recipe may be reduced by the amount of liquid color you add. It can be difficult, though, to get the amount of liquid color you add to be the same as the amount of water you subtract, and if you're making several different colors of icing out of one batch of buttercream, it's well-nigh impossible. A better method, therefore, is to use a combination of paste or powder and liquid. Use paste or powder color to turn your icing a light to medium shade, then add liquid to reach the desired darkness. This way, you get a deep color without having to use a lot of paste, powder, or liquid.

Coloring Royal:

Either paste or powder colors can be used for royal icing. Since neither affects the consistency of the icing, no adjustments need be made to the recipe. A water-base liquid color with no traces of oil would also be acceptable, but if your liquid color has any oils (many do) it will break down your royal icing and turn it into a runny, unusable mess. If you find a water-base liquid color with no oils, you can use it providing you reduce the amount of water called for in your recipe. If you're using an egg white (rather than meringue) recipe, which does not call for water, you must use paste or powder color.

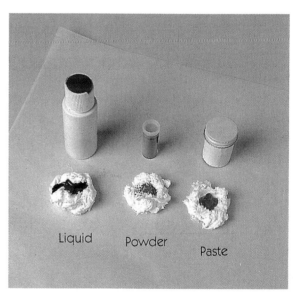

Liquid   Powder   Paste

Color Chart

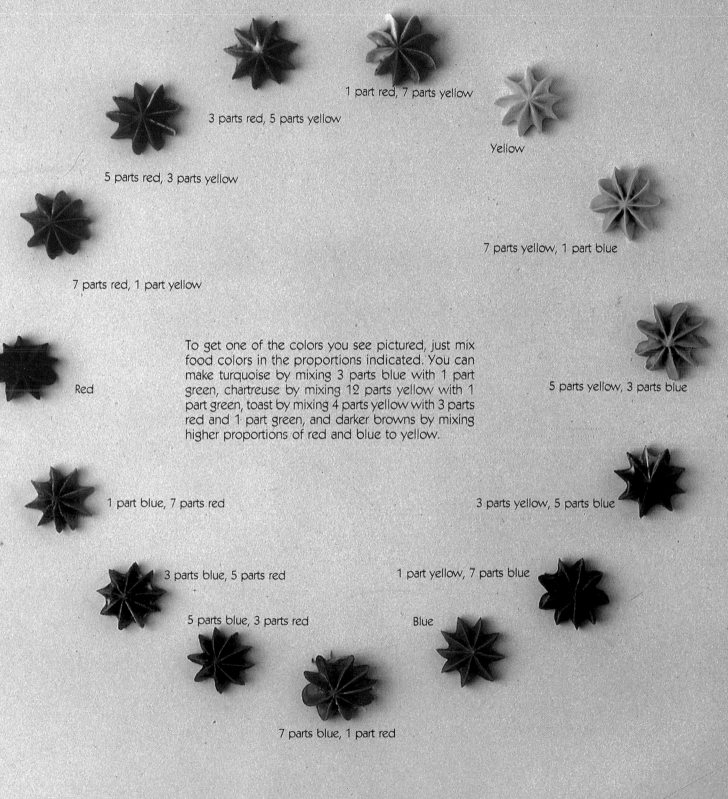

3 parts red, 5 parts yellow

1 part red, 7 parts yellow

Yellow

5 parts red, 3 parts yellow

7 parts yellow, 1 part blue

7 parts red, 1 part yellow

Red

To get one of the colors you see pictured, just mix food colors in the proportions indicated. You can make turquoise by mixing 3 parts blue with 1 part green, chartreuse by mixing 12 parts yellow with 1 part green, toast by mixing 4 parts yellow with 3 parts red and 1 part green, and darker browns by mixing higher proportions of red and blue to yellow.

5 parts yellow, 3 parts blue

1 part blue, 7 parts red

3 parts yellow, 5 parts blue

3 parts blue, 5 parts red

1 part yellow, 7 parts blue

5 parts blue, 3 parts red

Blue

7 parts blue, 1 part red

The Candy Counter

Gumballs

Gummy Bears

Licorice Diamonds

Red Licorice Squares

Gummy Seashells

Gummy Cola Bottles

Gumdrops

Red or Cinnamon Hots

Gummy Fish

Gummy Snakes

Jujus

Red and Black Licorice Sticks

Swiss Blackberry and Raspberry

Licorice Whips

Candy Corn

Chocolate Lentils

Hard Candy

Australian Crystalized Ginger

Sesame Candy

Candied Fruit Slices

California Crystalized Ginger

Jelly Beans

French Peppermints

Small Chocolate Squares

White and Dark Chocolate

Milk Chocolate, Dark Chocolate,
and Peanut Butter Chips

Edible Glitter

Gold and Silver Dragees

Dutch Chocolate Flakes

How To Make Money as a Cake Decorator

The Pricing Formula

When figuring out how much to charge for your cakes, there are 2 most important things to keep track of: how many hours you spend making the cake, and how much money you spend on ingredients.

The Time Factor

Like any 18-year-old kid trying to hold down a job at the neighborhood doughnut shop, or any Fortune 500 executive sitting on top of a pyramid of employees, you deserve a certain amount of money for each hour you work. The 18-year-old is likely to be satisfied with minimum wage. The executive probably earns twenty times that. What you deserve is sure to fall somewhere between the two, but only you can say exactly where. If you think you're more talented and experienced than the average person you're competing with, then you should charge more than your average competitor. If you're a beginning cake decorator and you don't feel confident that you're as good as most cake decorators in your geographical area, then you should charge less.

So let's say, after all this hemming and hawing, that you figure your skills are worth $6 an hour. And let's say it takes you 4 hours to bake and decorate a cake. How much time have you spent on the cake? $24 worth.

The Ingredient Factor

This is even simpler to figure than the time factor. Just keep track of the ingredients you use in the cake, and how much it cost you to buy them. Or, if you already had some of the ingredients in your kitchen, estimate how much it *would* have cost you if you had made a special trip to the store to get them. Remember, by the way, that you should never skimp on ingredients. Always buy the freshest and best you can find, unless the customer specifies otherwise. If your customers cared only about price, they would go to the supermarket and buy one of the mass-produced cakes available there.

So let's say you've spent $6 on the cake's ingredients. Now you've figured the two most important elements that determine how much you're going to charge for your cake. You've spent $24 of your time making the cake, and $6 of you money on the ingredients. So that means you charge $30 for the cake, right? Wrong! To arrive at the amount you should charge for your cake, take this figure and *triple* it. This gives you leeway to cover all the hidden costs and expenses you haven't taken into consideration. For example:
Time spent shopping for ingredients, cleaning up, taking orders, and doing general paper work.
Use of your kitchen, utensils, and fuel.
Time and ingredients wasted because of unforeseen accidents.

Costs and expenses like these make it essential that you triple your base figure—unless you want to *lose* money in the cake decorating business.

Of course, you'll always have to quote a price *before* the customer will agree to order the cake. Therefore, there's always a little bit of guesswork involved. The more experience you acquire, though, the more accurately and fairly your price will reflect your investment in time and money.

Costs Added on at the End

Finally, there are costs that should be added on to your figure, and not tripled. These include:
Delivery charge.
The cost of such items as separator plates, columns, and flowers for a wedding cake (charge the customer the same price you paid).
The cost of cartoon character specialty pans that you have to buy especially for the customer.

Verifying Your Arithmetic

If you're worried that the price you arrive at might be too high or too low, you can check your arithmetic by finding out what other cake decorators in your area are charging for an equivalent product. Say you figure that a 12" cake decorated with a basic puff border and made with quality ingredients should cost $90. Call up a few good bakeries and independent decorators and ask them what they would charge for the same size cake decorated the same way and made with the same ingredients. If there's a significant discrepancy, you know you have to readjust your price.

Rental of Reusable Items

In most cases, I strongly recommend *selling* the customer such items as columns and separator plates. Their cost usually isn't enough to justify all the extra paperwork. In some cases, though, you should give the customer the option of renting an item. Electric fountains for a wedding cake, for example, are relatively expensive, and the customer might be put off by the cost. The daily rental cost of such items should be about 1/5 of the amount you paid for them.

Favorite Recipes

What to Ask For in Advance

When the customer places the order, ask for a *non-refundable deposit* equivalent to ⅓ the cost of the cake. If the customer cancels the order at a later date, the deposit will at least cover the cost of any ingredients and materials you might have bought before cancellation. If the order isn't cancelled, the deposit allows you to use the *customer's* money to buy materials and ingredients, so that you don't run into any cash-flow problems.

What to Ask For Upon Delivery

Accept the remainder of payment for the cake when you deliver it. Also, ask for a security deposit for any items being rented to the customer, such as an electric fountain. The security deposit should be equivalent to the full replacement cost of the rented item. Also, you should receive payment for rental of the item, based on the number of days the customer anticipates keeping it. When it's returned, refund the security deposit.

Getting All the Information

When a customer places an order, *be sure* to write down all the following information:
The customer's name, address, and home and business phone.
The date for delivery of the cake.
The *exact* specifications of the cake: size and flavor of cake, type, flavor, and color of icing, flavor of filling, kind and color of flowers, and so on.
The quoted and agreed-upon price of the cake.
The amount of the deposit accepted upon receipt of order.
Terms for payment of the remainder of the price, including the details of a security deposit and cost of rental of any items.
Get all this information down *in writing,* and *be sure* to have the customer initial it. Give the customer a copy. That way, any later disagreement or misunderstanding can be resolved simply by referring to the written agreement.

Photographing Your Cakes

Always get a picture of your cake. Often, the cake will be photographed by the client (especially if it's a wedding or birthday cake), and if you get along well with him or her you could ask for a copy of one of the pictures. Or, you could take a snapshot yourself before delivery. It's always helpful to be able to show a customer photographs of cakes that *you* have made, rather than pictures of other people's cakes out of a book.

Here are some of my very favorite cake recipes I've collected over the years. You might like to try them for some of the projects in the book.

Remember that everybody's oven is different, and that you should always test the cake you're baking before assuming that it's done. Stick in a toothpick, and if it comes out wet, the cake needs more baking. An easy way to see if your oven is accurate, by the way, is to test it with an oven thermometer. If you set your oven for 350 degrees and your thermometer reads 300, you'll make things easier on yourself if you turn the dial on your oven closer to 400 degrees for a cake that needs to be baked at 350.

German Apple Cake

5-6 medium Winesap apples (if Winesaps are not available, use McIntosh or other cooking apples)
Granulated sugar
2 teaspoons cinnamon
3 cups all-purpose flour
1 cup oil
4 extra large eggs
½ cup orange juice
1 tablespoon baking powder
1 tablespoon vanilla
1 teaspoon salt
Core, peel, and chop the apples. Sprinkle with 5 tablespoons sugar and 2 teaspoons cinnamon, mix, and set aside.

Mix 2 cups sugar and all the other ingredients (except the apple mixture) in a large bowl. Pour half of the batter into a greased and floured 9" springform pan. Sprinkle in half of the apple mixture, then pour in the remaining batter, then sprinkle in the rest of the apple mixture.

Bake at 350 degrees for 1½ hours.

Plain Yellow Cake

1¼ cups cake flour, sifted
¾ cup granulated sugar
¾ cup solid shortening
6 tablespoons milk
2 large eggs
1¼ teaspoons baking powder
½ teaspoon salt
1 teaspoon vanilla
Place all the ingredients in order into the bowl of an electric mixer. Mix at low speed for 2 minutes and then at high speed for 3 minutes. Pour into greased and floured cake pans (I recommend 2 9" x 2" pans, or 1 9" x 3"). Bake at 350 degrees for 30 to 40 minutes.

German Pound Cake

1 cup granulated sugar
½ cup room temperature butter
1¾ cups cake flour, sifted
½ cup milk
3 large or extra large egg yolks
1 teaspoon vanilla
¾ teaspoon baking powder
  Pinch salt

In the bowl of an electric mixer, beat sugar and butter at high speed until light and fluffy. Add rest of ingredients at while mixing at low speed, scraping the sides of the bowl with a rubber spatula. Then, beat at high speed for 5 to 6 minutes. Pour into greased and floured pans. Bake at 350 degrees for 1 hour.

Sponge Cake

8 eggs
1½ cups granulated sugar
1½ cups strudel or all-purpose flour
2 teaspoons baking powder
1 teaspoon salt
1 teaspoon vanilla

In the bowl of an electric mixer, beat eggs at high speed until foamy. Gradually sprinkle in the sugar while mixing, and when all the sugar is added beat about 8 minutes, until the mixture is fluffy and very pale yellow. Gradually add rest of ingredients while mixing at low speed. Pour batter into greased pans lined with wax or parchment paper. Bake at 350 degrees for approximately 20 minutes.

Dominican Yellow Cake

Dominican Yellow Cake is becoming more and more popular here in the States. When you buy a Dominican cake in an Hispanic bakery, you usually pay $20 to $25 per pound. This doesn't mean the piece of cake weighs a pound, but that it has a pound of butter, a pound of flour, a pound of sugar, and a dozen eggs.

1 lb. room temperature unsalted butter
8 extra large eggs, separated
4 extra large eggs, unseparated
1 lb. (4 cups) cake flour, sifted
3 tablespoons baking powder
2 tablespoons Dominican vanilla (if you can't find
    Dominican vanilla, use 3 tablespoons regular vanilla)
½ cup milk
1 lb (about 2 cups) granulated sugar
  Rind of 1 lemon, grated
  Pinch of salt

Cream the butter and sugar with an electric mixer set at high speed. One at a time, add the 8 egg yolks. Then add the 4 whole eggs, one at a time, beating briefly after each addition. Turn the mixer to low speed, and add the sifted cake flour. Add the baking powder, vanilla, milk, and the grated lemon rind. Refrigerate.

Put the 8 egg whites and pinch of salt into a bowl (preferably copper or, if you don't have a copper bowl, glass). Beat at high speed until mixture is peaked and stiff but not dry.

Remove yellow mixture from refrigerator. Gently fold half the yellow mixture into the egg whites, and then fold this mixture into the remaining yellow mixture.

Pour into greased and floured cake pans. Bake at 350 degrees for approximately 40 minutes, or until center is dry.

Note: Try to avoid opening your oven door often while this cake is baking. Like a soufflé, the Dominican Cake is temperamental, and is best left alone and undisturbed while in the oven.

Pineapple Filling

This is the perfect filling for my Dominican Yellow Cake.
½ cup granulated sugar
6 tablespoons cornstarch
¼ teaspoon salt
1½ cups canned pineapple juice
4 tablespoons butter
2 tablespoons lemon juice
1½ cups crushed pineapple

In a 2-quart saucepan, mix together sugar, cornstarch, and salt. Gradually stir in pineapple juice. Add the butter and lemon juice and heat to a boil, stirring constantly. Boil mixture for about 2 minutes until mixture is smooth and thickened. Add crushed pineapple. Mix by hand. Refrigerate for 2 to 3 hours.

Note: You can also make this recipe with ¾ cup crushed pineapple and ¾ cup mandarin oranges, instead of 1½ cups pineapple. Or, any crushed or finely chopped fruit may be substituted, as can any juice be substituted for the pineapple juice called for in my pineapple filling recipe. Always be sure that the juice you use goes well with the fruit.

Indonesian Yellow Cake

1 cup butter or margarine
9 extra large eggs
1½ cups granulated sugar
1½ cups cake flour, sifted
1 teaspoon vanilla

In a heavy saucepan, melt the butter or margarine. In a large mixing bowl, beat the eggs and sugar at high speed until smooth. Add flour all at once. Stir until blended. Add vanilla. Add melted butter or margarine and stir.

Pour into greased and floured pans (I recommend a 13" x 9" sheet cake pan, or 10" round). Bake at 350 degrees for 15–20 minutes or until golden.

Rosie's Rocky Roth

½ cup butter, melted
2 cups granulated sugar
2 cups cake flour, sifted
1 tablespoon baking soda
1 tablespoon baking powder
¾ cup unsweetened cocoa powder, preferably Dutch-process
1 cup milk
1 cup hot coffee
2 eggs
1 teaspoon vanilla
½ cup walnut pieces

Going in order, one at a time, mix all the above ingredients in the bowl of an electric mixer. Beat slowly after each addition.

Pour into greased and floured pans (I recommend 3 6" x 3" pans, or 2 8" x 3"). Bake at 325 degrees for 25–30 minutes.

Note: Although this is a rich chocolate cake, it may be frosted if desired. I like to use 1 lb. semi-sweet chocolate, melted in the top of a double boiler, and poured over the cake.

Larry's Lively Lemon Cake

½ lb. butter, softened
1½ cups granulated sugar
6 eggs, separated
¾ cup lemon juice
1 teaspoon vanilla
2½ cups cake flour, sifted
2 teaspoons baking powder
¼ teaspoon salt

In the bowl of an electric mixer, beat butter and sugar until creamy. Add egg yolks one at a time, beating after each addition. Add lemon juice and vanilla. Gradually add cake flour, baking powder, and salt. In a separate bowl (preferably copper), beat egg whites until they form peaks. Carefully fold half of the egg whites into the yellow mixture, then fold the entire mixture into the remaining egg whites. *Do not beat.*

Pour into greased and floured pans (I recommend 3 6" x 3" pans, or 2 8" x 3"). Bake at 350 degrees for 45 minutes, or until a tester comes out clean.

Lemon Frosting

(Perfect for my lemon cake.)
4 cups confectioners sugar, sifted
¾ cup solid vegetable shortening
¾ cups unsalted butter, softened
2 tablespoons water
2 tablespoons lemon essence
Pinch of salt

In the bowl of an electric mixer, blend all the ingredients at low speed. Then beat at high speed for 5 to 7 minutes.

English Fruitcake

The marzipan covering I show you how to make in the "Alternative Icings" chapter goes great on this fruitcake.

2 cups strudel or all-purpose flour
6 ounces room temperature unsalted butter
¼ cup light brown sugar
3 extra large eggs
3 tablespoons rum
Zest of 1 lemon
½ teaspoon baking powder
½ teaspoon ground cinnamon
½ teaspoon powdered cloves
12 ounces diced mixed candied fruits
8 ounces light raisins
8 ounces dark raisins
4 ounces currants
4 ounces yellow, red, and green candied pineapple (reserve 1 piece of each color for garnish)
4 ounces red and green glacéed cherries (save 6 of each color for garnish)
2 ounces whole blanched almonds (save 18 pieces for garnish)
2 ounces diced candied citron
2 ounces diced lemon peel
2 ounces diced orange peel
2 ounces diced glacéed apricot halves
2 ounces walnut pieces (optional)
2 ounces pecan halves (optional)
Dark rum

In a 10-quart mixing bowl, mix flour, butter, sugar, eggs, rum, lemon, baking powder, cinnamon, and cloves until creamy with a wire whip. Add slowly, stirring after each addition, candied mixed fruits, light raisins, dark raisins, currants, pineapple, cherries, almonds, citron, lemon peel, orange peel, and apricots (and the walnuts and pecans, if desired).

Grease and flour a loaf pan approximately 12" x 4¼" x 3¼". Line pan with wax or parchment paper. Pour batter into pan, and garnish the top with the pineapples, cherries, and almonds you set aside. Bake at 325 degrees for 1½ hours. Allow to cool.

Remove from pan and pour dark rum over the fruitcake. Wrap in cheesecloth, plastic wrap, and foil, in that order. Refrigerate overnight. Unwrap it the next day, pour some more rum over it, and then wrap it back up again and put it back in the fridge. Repeat the next day.

This fruitcake can be stored in the refrigerator, or in a tin. It should always be kept wrapped in the cheesecloth, plastic wrap, and foil. It'll stay fresh for months.

Where to Get Unusual Items

Mail-Order Resources

Mail-Order Resources